the
TRUTH
about
GUYs

the TRUTH about GUYS

One Guy Reveals What Every Girl Should Know

Chad Eastham

TRANSIT®

www.TransitBooks.com
A Division of Thomas Nelson, Inc.
www.ThomasNelson.com

THE TRUTH ABOUT GUYS: ONE GUY REVEALS WHAT EVERY GIRL SHOULD KNOW

Copyright © 2006 by Chad Eastham

Published in Nashville, Tennessee, by Tommy Nelson®, a Division of Thomas Nelson, Inc. Visit us on the Web at www.tommynelson.com.

Scripture quotations are from *The Holy Bible, New Century Version*®, copyright © 2005 by Thomas Nelson, Inc.

Every effort has been made to credit any and all sources of information throughout this book. If by some small chance a source has been excluded, we will gladly add it in all future printings.

Library of Congress Cataloging-in-Publication Data

Eastham, Chad, 1980-
    The truth about guys : one guy reveals what every girl should know / by Chad Eastham.
      p. cm.
    Includes bibliographical references.
    ISBN-10: 1-4003-0968-9 (alk. paper)
    ISBN-13: 978-1-4003-0968-9
    1. Man-woman relationships—Religious aspects—Christianity. 2. Teenage boys. 3. Adolescence. I. Title.
    BT705.8.E27 2006
    248.8'3—dc22

2006021279

Printed in the United States of America

06 07 08 09 10 LBM 9 8 7 6 5 4 3 2 1

For Laura . . .
Every time you smile, you steal my heart.

To Ryan, Taylor, and Kyle . . .
You are small angels. Your uncle loves you.

Love each other like brothers and sisters.
Give each other more honor than
you want for yourselves.

—Romans 12:10

Contents

The Truth About Me 1

Introduction: The Wonderful, Weird World of Guys . . . 3

Part 1: Girls Are Spaghetti

1. Girls Rule 9
2. Until You Like Yourself,
   Nobody Else Can Either 15
3. Your Noodles—Our Boxes 21
4. Mirror, Mirror 29
5. Miss Magnet 41
6. Treasure or Target? 47
7. Who's Your Daddy? 57

Part 2: Guys Are Waffles

8. The Five Toughest Questions Girls Ask
   (And How to Answer Them) 69
9. What We Don't Say 77
10. Guys Feel Like Impostors 83
11. Guys and Commitment 93
12. What Guys Really Want 103
13. Guys Have Secrets 113
14. Dating Advice from Guys 121

Part 3: Barbie and GI Joe

15. Why They Aren't Friends 135
16. Extra! Extra! Hear All About It! 147
17. The Reality of Sex 157
18. This Thing Called Love 173
19. Dude Bonding 183
20. Filters and Pressure Gauges 189

Part 4: Other Guy-Girl Things

21. More Stuff Girls Want to Know! 199
22. Leaving Guy-ville 209
23. Unbelievable . . . but TRUE! 215

Notes 221

The Truth About Me . . .

I will always remember sitting alone in my dimly lit, padded security room. I was angry and crying after being restrained on the cold floor. I'd been taken to the third most intensive drug and alcohol treatment facility in the country after a hearing. I remember thinking, *How did I get here? How did I wind up in some crummy room that's anywhere but "Happy-ville" for a teenager?* I was supposed to be laughing, dating, hanging out with the guys, and being a normal kid.

Some bad choices and lousy life circumstances had led me there. It felt like I had reached the end. I didn't realize that it was just the beginning.

I spent just over a year there, and during that time I realized that I wasn't the only person who wanted to feel normal and accepted. It was there, of all places, that I learned that people *don't* have everything all figured out. It didn't matter where we came from; all of us longed for something more . . . things like good friendships, great relationships, and a life that makes sense.

I wish that people would have just talked to me back then in a way that I could understand. I wish they would have talked *with* me and not *at* me. I would have listened.

A short time later, I was sent to talk with kids at juvenile detention centers. I realized that's how they felt too. Then as I spoke at camps, churches, high schools, colleges, and many other places, I found the same thing to be true. We want people to be real with us, to understand us, and to talk with us.

Unfortunately, most adults don't give teens a lot of credit. The fact is, though, teenagers need people to talk with them in the language of the world they live in. People came into my life when I was a teenager and told me I was important. They talked *with* me, and I listened. It saved my life. They helped me see that because I was created by a God who loves me, I am valuable and have plenty to offer this world. I wish every teen would know this truth.

We are valuable because God made each of us unique— as guys, as girls, as individuals. Once we believe that, we can better understand how to relate to one another.

The more we know about one another, the better off we all are. That's why I wrote this book, so that in some small way you might better understand how guys tend to think and act, so that you can make better decisions about how to respond to the guys in your life.

I hope you know that you're valuable to God and others no matter what your life circumstances. I hope you know that you belong. You fit in. You're normal, and you can have a life of meaning and purpose.

I've also learned something else about teens. Eventually, you are going to make your own decisions. My prayer is that you will make good ones. Not because you're supposed to, but because you can. Life has a lot to offer. I hope you'll squeeze all the good you can from it.

Thanks for taking a moment to get to know me. I wish you all the best in your journey.

—Chad Eastham

The Wonderful, Weird World of Guys

Since you're reading this book, you may be wondering about guys. Who in the world are we? Why do we do the things we do? What makes us do stuff that seems so goofy and makes no sense?

You're not alone. Girls wonder about guys . . . along with a million other things. How do you find the truth about guys?

The truth, the whole truth, and nothing but the truth about guys can't be summed up in a few words. There is no simple formula with easy answers to all of your questions. Especially when your head and heart are probably screaming with millions of them. Am I right? Questions like:

- Why do guys try to act tough?
- Why do guys think it's cool to fight?
- Why do guys always do gross stuff?
- Why do guys think and talk about sex so much?
- Why are some guys such jerks?
- Why do guys care so much about what girls look like?
- Why don't guys like to talk about their feelings?
- What does a guy really want in a girl?
- Why are guys so different from girls?

While this book won't answer every question you have about guys, *The Truth About Guys* will explore some of the stuff about us that you may not realize. We'll dig deeper into the real whys and why-nots behind the baffling, and often silly, things guys do.

Don't just sit back and relax. If you want to know the truth about guys, you'd better be asking all of the same questions about *yourself*. It's not about catching a guy, bashing either gender, or changing who you are. None of that works in the long run anyway. This book is about understanding who guys are, and, more important, understanding yourself in relation to them.

> Nobody will ever win the battle of the sexes. There's too much fraternizing with the enemy.
>
> —Henry Kissinger

I just turned twenty-five. I guess that makes me an "old man" now, but I really enjoy it. I can now see a little further down the road than I could when I was a teen. Yet I'm still young enough to understand what teens are going through. Over the years I've been a counselor and a camp director, and I've run youth organizations in and out of schools. I really care about what guys and girls go through in their teen years.

Although I'm a guy and you're a girl, in the end we have to understand not only ourselves but each other. The more we understand each other, the better off we are when it comes to making things work. If girls understand some basic stuff about guys, it may just make life more manageable and even a whole lot more fun! That's what this book is about.

Let's get started, shall we?

If men and women are to

understand each other,

to enter into each other's

nature with mutual sympathy,

and to become capable of

genuine comradeship, the

foundation must be

laid in youth.

—Henry Ellis

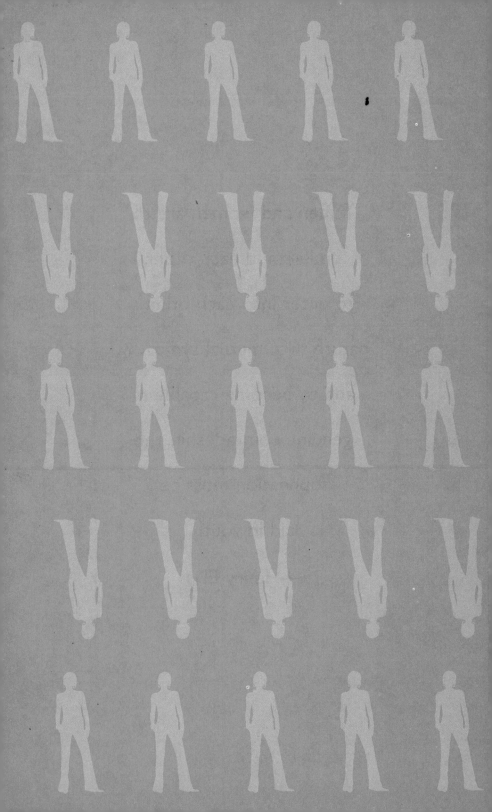

Girls Are Spaghetti

I came to give life—
life in all its fullness.

—John 10:10

1

Girls Rule

There is a woman at the
beginning of all great things.

—Alphonse de Lamartine

As Kurt walked down the hall of his high school, he turned the corner and headed for his locker. It was hard to miss what had been done. Streamers, balloons, and a huge, glittery sign screamed HAPPY BIRTHDAY from his locker. Tracy had obviously remembered.

Sure, he felt a little flushed as he fiddled with the lock and felt the stares of the kids around him, but inside he felt pretty good. As he opened the door, even more surprises were waiting. Tickets to the Cubs game were taped to the back of the locker door, and a large plastic container of homemade chocolate chip cookies were waiting to be eaten. Excellent. Any embarrassment that he may have had to deal with from the decorations had just been offset by the cookies. He reached in and took a bite! ■

Guys Like Girls—Really!

I can't recall a story about a guy baking cookies for himself. We just don't do that. As much as we love cookies—and believe me, we love cookies—most of us guys just don't bake them and give them away on our own.

Without girls, guys would be a mess! You do all kinds of things that are sweet, kind, and wonderful. All those girly traits you have make a guy's world complete. The fact is, *girls rule!*

> Mountains are spectacular because they are mountains. There doesn't need to be any explanation for why they captivate us. They just do. We look at them in awe. Girls are even more intriguing than mountains, because that's the way God made them. And guys would much rather look at girls than mountains.

Why? Because you smile prettier than we do, and you smell way better than we do. There are probably a few hundred other reasons as well. Don't worry. We'll get to a lot of them eventually.

You are a girl. That's all it takes. I'm not sure a lot of you understand that you are incredibly valuable and worthy simply because God created you.

I spend a lot of time hanging out with students. I speak to them at schools, talk with them, do research about them, and read their letters. Basically, they give me a glimpse into what their lives are like.

As much as guys love sports and music, hanging out with other guys, getting dirty, lighting things on fire, or lifting weights, there is something that will always appeal to us much more than all of that—YOU! We like girls, love girls, need girls, and, in case I haven't mentioned it yet, we like the way girls smell. Guys know that everything is better because of girls. Girls are the balance to the dirty, unorganized, and violent world that would exist if only guys were in charge.

TOTALLY TREASURED

Here are just a few things that most guys love about most girls:

- Girls are dependable.
- Girls are great listeners.
- Girls are more sensitive than guys.
- Girls make us feel strong.
- Girls put so much effort into everything they do.
- Girls are organized.
- Girls can do lots of stuff at once.

Girls Are Cool

There is something I've observed about girls in the classroom, in youth groups, at football games, at restaurants, or at the mall. Girls are really cool. No kidding, you really are. Sure, you're a little silly sometimes, but you're fun and sweet and hilarious. Actually, guys are cool too; don't get me wrong. It's just that guys, especially between the ages of thirteen and eighteen, try so hard to be macho. They can't help it.

Now that I'm a little older, here's what I see: guys and girls are distinctly *different*. God chose to make women unique, and there is nothing else like them in all of his creation. Men have written about women in love poems, novels, poetry, and music throughout time—yet our fascination with women never really changes! Women stir up wonder, amazement, and pure mystery in the very fabric of men. In some small way, we are trying to capture your true nature, which can never fully be realized. Still, we keep trying and always will.

Guys have always been completly and utterly fascinated with girls! If the mountains and oceans are the peaks of God's earthly creation, then women are by far his best creation when it comes to living things.

Here's a little secret: God sees you as his beautiful creation. He's the one who said, "It is not good for the man to be alone" (Genesis 2:18). So he made women. No guy can make you into anything more beautiful than God already has. Our job is to affirm the worth you have already been given.

Be a friend
to thyself,
and others will
be so too.

—Thomas Fuller

2

Until You Like Yourself, Nobody Else Can Either

I didn't belong as a kid, and that always bothered me. If I'd only known that one day my differentness would be an asset, then my early life would have been much easier.

—Bette Midler

What's wrong, Jamie?" her mom asked as she came home from school in a huff. Jamie's face was flushed and wore a scowl.

"Wrong? Wrong? Let's see . . . I can't stand my droopy hair. I've gained seven pounds. I don't have anything new to wear, so I look like a dork. I didn't make the cheerleading squad. And now I've got two huge zits on my face! It's no wonder Jimmy Kennedy doesn't like me!"

"Oh, sweetheart," her mom replied. "You're a beautiful girl. If Jimmy doesn't see that, then he doesn't deserve to go out with you."

Jamie looked at her mom and rolled her eyes. "I knew you wouldn't understand," she said. ■

What Do You Know?

Girls really do rule in a lot of ways. It's true. Just in case you have any doubts, check this out:

- Girls usually aren't fashion blind. You wear stuff that looks great together, including your shoes. Your bedrooms are cute, coordinated, and everything matches. This is utterly baffling to most guys.

- Girls are often more honest. You aren't afraid to feel things, speak from your hearts, and you sometimes learn to trust more easily.

- The U.S. Soccer Women's National Team has won two World Cups, and the men have won zero.

- Girls have more clothing choices. Girls can wear shirts, pants, dresses, shorts, skirts, and shoes . . . in four million combinations of ways.

- Girls often motivate the guys you like to do all sorts of things guys normally wouldn't do—take a shower, look you right in the eyes when talking to you, write you love songs, buy gifts, remember special occasions, and even try to save the world!

- Girls usually grow up to be mothers.

- Girls are more likely than guys to dance great, and you're almost always willing to teach us how to do it.

- Girls giggle, jump around, and get really excited with each other for no reason. Do you enjoy life more, or does it just seem like it?

- Girls usually pay attention to the little things, which makes everyday life feel more special.

HERE'S A SECRET:

Here's a secret: the more comfortable you are with yourself, the more comfortable you are with others. I'll probably say this over and over again, but it's because you really need to know it. The more comfortable you are with yourself, the more comfortable you are with others.

We can talk about all the reasons in the world that girls are great. But the individual, unique *you* God created may be tall, short, thin, or heavy; pearl, oval, boxy, or pencil shaped; brunette, blonde, or redheaded; Asian, African, Caucasian, or alien! You might be outgoing, shy, an ace student, or one who has to study twice as much as your friends. You may be a superathlete or a klutz. You get the idea.

None of that, or anything else, really matters until you are comfortable with yourself for who God made you to be. Psalm 139:14 says that God made you in "an amazing and wonderful way." Trust God's words about you, even when you feel bad about yourself.

You're got to know that you are special, because you are good, funny, smart, kind, goofy, smiley, silly, mysterious, passionate, creative, and a billion other wonderful and zany traits that God gave you. Seeing yourself as God sees you will help others, including guys, see how wonderful you are! ▼

Maybe this sounds a little trite, like something your mom and dad told you, but it's the truth. You can circle the globe for answers, but the only way you can become comfortable with yourself is by trusting that what God says about you in his Word is true. Nothing in this book matters as much as you accepting the fact that God has made you as something terrific.

Guys like girls who know that they are valuable. That doesn't mean stuck-up, trendy, or sexy, but *valuable*.

> You made my whole being; you formed me in my mother's body. I praise you because you made me in an amazing and wonderful way.
>
> —Psalm 139:13–14

Girls with a poor self-image often *don't* end up happily ever after. Sure, sometimes things happen and life turns out great. God has an awesome way of showing us love, redemption, forgiveness, and real value through our friendships and relationships. But God already made each one of us unique and beautiful. It's up to us to embrace who we are and to love ourselves so that our inner being can shine out to others. That's what makes us loveable.

On Your Mark, Get Set, Go!

The starting point in all of this is *you*! The God of the entire universe created *you*. You are *his*. He loves you just the way you are. Do you see yourself the way he sees you? The Bible says God doesn't look at your outward appearance; he looks at your heart (1 Samuel 16:7). That means what you think is more important to God than what you look like.

The fact is, though, what you think of yourself will determine everything else about how others see and think of you. When you are comfortable on the inside, it changes everything about how you look and relate to others, including *guys!*

Here are a few questions to get you thinking about where your starting point is:

What do people think of you when they meet you? Do they think you care about them?

> When we seek to discover the best in others, we somehow bring out the best in ourselves.
>
> —William Arthur Ward

What are the three best things about you? How would you rank your beauty, intelligence, and humor from one (being bad) to ten (being great)?

Are you awesome, cool, and fun to hang out with? Are you more of a flirt or a friend? Are you confident or just faking it? Are you selfish and self-centered, or are other guys and girls important to you?

What does a guy have to do to earn your attention? Is it easy or difficult for others to get your attention?

What are the three most important things in your life? What are some of your greatest achievements? What do you feel most comfortable with about yourself?

Do you allow yourself to be loved the way God says you are to be loved?

If you don't know the answers to most of these questions, that's okay. Like most girls, you really *do* have a lot to learn about yourself.

Guys tend to be more enthralled and excited about girls who are secure about their own worth. Guys can't create your value; we can only appreciate it. You have to be the starting point. You have to know that God loves you, or you can't love yourself—and nobody else can love you either. And the cool thing is that you don't have to guess about whether or not God loves you. It's clear in the Bible that he does! (See Psalm 59:17; John 3:16; John 16:27; Colossians 3:12; and 1 Thessalonians 1:4.)

You have to love the real you—the entire package that God bundled up in creating you to be someone so unique and special that you could never be anyone else, no matter how hard you try.

GUY TIP:

If you want to know what you can do for guys, you can start by focusing on yourself. It's not about how you look, how much you weigh, or how much attention you get from us. When you discover yourself, guys are free to discover you too. When you realize just how great you are, then guys will also. The truth is, we really want you to be great! It makes us want to be great too.

3

Your Noodles—Our Boxes

She said, 'Hi, Kristi, good to see ya.' But I don't like the way she said it, 'cause I don't think she actually meant it. The sound of her voice reminded me of the way that Julie talks in class, and she called me fat last month behind my back. And I know she did. Besides, who is she to be saying that in the first place? Plus she never shuts up, and she's always talking about herself and sticking her chest out and flirting with people, including my boyfriend, Mark. And don't even get me started about Mark, because what's his deal anyway? I could smack him for acting like he totally doesn't know she is trying to flirt with him, 'cause you know he does. I saw him laughing when she was talking to him in the hallway, and it made me mad because she was wearing the same skirt I had just bought. And he said something about it to her, and he never even noticed it when I wore it."

A guy's response to that: "What?" ■

Waffles and Noodles

Some guys were over at my place one night, and there was lots of yelling: "Hit him! Beat him! Make him bleed!"

Don't worry. It was on the television. We were watching a huge title fight for the middleweight boxing championship of the world. And just so you know, we didn't use fancy plates, none of us smelled good, no one thought to tell anyone to bring something "fun" to eat, and absolutely nobody was getting their hair braided. We were eating, laughing, and yelling at a television screen as though the fighters in the ring could hear us. I'm sure my neighbors could.

When dudes get together, we pretty much get pizza. It's easy, and we don't have to do anything except walk to the door, hand over some money, put down the box, pick up food with our hands, and shove it into our mouths. And we usually wind up burning the top of our mouths trying to shove the whole piece in.

> Listen to your mom, sister, or girlfriends talk, and you'll hear something like, "I feel bored. Let's go to the mall." Then check it out with your dad, brothers, or the guys at school. You'll hear something like, "I think that was a great show" or, "I think that's the dumbest thing I've ever seen."

Well, you get the idea. It was a very "dude" evening. But as I sat there, I noticed how the guys were talking with each other. Something funny occurred to me. Somewhere I'd heard that even the nouns and verbs people use can show whether or not they have a male or female brain. And sure enough, not one time did someone say the word *feel* or begin a sentence with,

"I feel . . ." Nah. We were all spouting opinionated statements, starting each one with, "I think . . ."

The fact is, guys mostly talk about what we *think* and girls mostly talk about what you *feel*.

Why? Because guys' brains work like all those little boxes on a waffle, and girls are pretty much spaghetti heads—a mixture of heartfelt, emotional, and wonderful squiggly noodles capable of going this way and that in the course of one single sentence. It's all because of the way God made guys and girls and the way we are wired.

It's important to understand how and why we're different. For example, guys tend to appreciate compassion in girls more than any other traits. Girls tend to appreciate guys' strength, dependability, and ability to protect. Now all you have to do is try to figure out how that balance works.

I read about the concept of women being like spaghetti and men being like waffles in a book by Bill and Pam Farrel that came out several years ago. It's called *Men Are Like Waffles—Women Are Like Spaghetti*, of course![1] It made perfect sense to me. That analogy helps us understand the whole guy-girl thing better than anything I've ever heard.

Noodle-licious

A guy's waffle brain is a lot more compartmentalized than yours. We tend to spend more time in the compartments we're good at, rather than the ones where we stink.

Take for example . . . getting ready in the morning. I'm serious. If you want to see how guys' and girls' brains function very differently, consider the morning routine.

Most guys get up, shower, and wolf down a few bowls of cereal, a couple of eggs, and several toaster pastries. We glance around the room for the cleanest pair of jeans we can find, search for a T-shirt that we typically find under our math homework, and peek in the hamper to see if yesterday's socks don't smell too bad. We brush our teeth and run a comb quickly through our hair, if there's enough time. If not, no big deal.

Most girls, on the other hand, get up much earlier to truly "prepare." After you shower, you spend a lot of time in front of the mirror. Every part of your makeup has to be just perfect, and I'm not going to pretend to know what's involved in each part. Then there's the hair. From what I hear, it's usually not curly enough, not straight enough, not long enough, or not short enough—whatever it is, it's definitely not enough something.

Then you eat what I'd call a tidbit of breakfast. Perhaps you'll eat one-half of a muffin, one-half of a piece of toast, or one-half of a grapefruit. It's usually one-half of something, a bite of something, or a taste of something.

Then it's time to get dressed. If you haven't thought things out the night before, you have to consider what kind of day it will be, the weather, who you're going to see, and what you're going to do. Then you have to decide pants or skirt, shorts or capris, long sleeves or T-shirt, sweater or jacket. Plus what you look like in each one, if the color works, and if it makes you look too heavy. There are too many combinations to mention, so let's just say that when you do decide, you're not done! What about shoes? That's another issue altogether.

Wait! We haven't even touched on accessories. Am I right? Earrings, necklaces, bracelets, watches, rings, clips, belts, ribbons, bows, and umpteen other things I've missed.

Add to that whatever perfume is best for the day's activities, and maybe you're ready to head out the door.

I'm not saying this is true of every girl, and it may not be true of you, but there are a lot of girls out there spending a *lot* of time in the morning making these really tough, life-altering decisions. And these are the decisions that, for a lot of girls, will determine if they have a great day or a horrible day, whether or not they pay attention in class, and even whether or not they are friendly to other kids at school. I've known girls who wore what they thought were the wrong shoes with the wrong shirt and, as a result, skipped the afternoon of classes! Really. I've never known a guy who thought like that.

This might be a good way to see how differently guys and girls think about and view our bodies and self-image. It starts with all that noodle-wiring upstairs.

Reading Between the Lines

Your wiring is more connected than ours. You don't have the same compartments with walls separating all your life categories.

Girls' brains are filled with little intersections that allow quick movement from one topic to another. Guys like to stay on just one road at a time. Guys like a simple event. Girls can process between one event and another easily. That's because you are great at multitasking. Guys aren't as good at keeping track of lots of things simultaneously.

GIRLS: Do your homework, watch television, paint your toenails, look through a catalog, and talk on the phone—all at once.

GUYS: Like to play video games. That's it. Or watch a football game. That's it. Or eat. That's it. One activity at a time. All-consuming.

Doing all the things girls do at once would give guys a nosebleed. But it's not anyone's fault. It's just how girls work. Girls can include emotional, spiritual, logical, and relational issues all in one conversation. This is confusing to guys who have trouble jumping from one box to another. We can end up baffled and overwhelmed.

But remember, neither girls nor guys designed themselves or their own brains or how those brains work. Read the first part of the book of Genesis. When God created Adam, he took one long look at him and said, basically, "Uh-oh. This isn't going to work. This dude can't be alone. He needs something. Let's see, what is it?" Then God said, "It is not good for the man to be alone. I will make a helper who is right for him" (Genesis 2:18). I'm sure that God knew what he was doing!

Go Slow . . . Guys Are Trying!

You girls have all kinds of really cool things that are unique to you. Your brain is connected in many more ways than ours. One example is how you talk to others.

Your ability to communicate is really cool. I can't always follow what you're saying, but when I can, it's cool. People's brains are divided into two simple hemispheres, the left and the right. The left side of the brain is logical. The right side is emotional. Each one accounts for many of the differences between girls and guys. When guys talk, it usually involves only the left hemisphere of the brain. But for girls, both the logical and the emotional sides work together at the same time. This makes most of you more skilled at verbal communication than we tend to be. Ever notice how girls have such a good memory about conversations? "Don't you remember? We talked about that!"

That's because you're better at pairing up words and concepts. Because of that, sometimes it's hard for girls to understand that guys don't approach talking—or even life—in the same way you do.

GUY TIPS:

- *Be patient.* Go slow with guys. We're trying. We may just follow slower than you want us to.
- *Be understanding.* Don't think guys don't care or aren't trying if we don't talk as much or as fast as you do.
- *Be sensitive.* Guys will do better if you clarify the point than if we have to guess what it is.

4

Mirror, Mirror

God has given you one face,
and you make yourselves another.

—Shakespeare, *Hamlet*

Two girls were getting ready to start their first day at a new high school. When the first girl sat down with her counselor, she asked, "What are the kids like at this school?"

The counselor asked, "What were they like where you came from?"

"They were terrible," the girl answered. "They were judgmental and untrustworthy, and they were mean to me!"

"Ah," said the counselor. "You will find them to be pretty much the same here, I'm afraid." Then he sent her to her first class.

The second girl sat down with the counselor. She asked the counselor the exact same question, and he responded by asking her what the people were like at her old school. ▼

"They were fine," she said. "They were pretty nice to me as long as I was nice to them. Most kids were fun, thoughtful, and just trying to get by like the rest of us."

The counselor responded, "Excellent. Well, you will find them to be the same way here." ■

Your Mirror

Like it or not, there is a simple truth in your life: **how you view yourself is going to determine how other people view you.** As they say, life is 10 percent what happens to us and 90 percent how we deal with it. When it comes to what you see in the mirror, it's the same way.

What do you see when you look in the mirror? What do other people see? Is it the same image that God had in mind when he created you? Is it the person your mom, dad, grandma, and aunt always tell you that you are? Do you see

> Behavior is a mirror in which everyone displays his own image.
>
> —Johann Wolfgang von Goethe

yourself as loveable, beautiful, and as someone people want to appreciate? Or do you think all that stuff is just cheesy?

Beauty comes from the inside, right? If only it were that easy! Wouldn't it be nice if simply knowing that truth would help you love yourself more? If it would help take away the worry about how you look? If it would help you know that it doesn't matter so much what other people think about you and that the only opinion that counts is God's?

The fact is, I don't think most teens, especially girls, feel that way at all.

In a recent study of eleven- to seventeen-year-old females, the number one desire was to *be thinner!*[1] Not smarter, taller, funnier, kinder, or a better listener. In fact, none of the findings had to do with girls wanting to change anything other than their physical features. That's really messed up, and we all know it. But what are we supposed to do about it?

> Look in a mirror and one thing is sure; what we see is not who we are.
>
> —Richard Bach

What you do about what you see in the mirror now will have dramatic effects on your future. You can wind up in a lot of exciting places and in some really great relationships, but they won't be determined by the classes you take, the grades you get, or the hairstyle you choose. They're going to be decided by what you see when you look in that mirror.

If you think you're great, so will your friends. Plus, you'll tend to think they're great too. You won't be judging yourself, so you won't need to judge others. **If you don't think much of yourself, your friends—whether they're guys or girls—won't either.**

Every morning when you wake up and look in the mirror, what you see in that mirror has very little to do with what you really look like, believe it or not. It does, however, have everything to do with what you look like to *yourself*.

You're probably wondering what that means. Let's try to break it down into something that makes sense, rather than having it sound like some goofy pep talk that you couldn't care less about.

Chick Schools

I was speaking at an all-girls school in Cincinnati, and everything was going along fine. I was getting a lot of the same questions about sex, teen relationships, and so on. I was about to finish up for the day when the girls started asking questions like, "Why do guys just care about what girls look like?" and, "Do you know how hard it is to look perfect for guys all the time?" I realized then that many of you don't feel great about yourselves. The good thing is, though, you aren't afraid to talk about it.

HERE'S A SECRET:

That's entirely different for guys. We don't try to perfect our exterior as much as girls do. And you know what? We are probably better off for it. We somehow sense that this has a negative outcome and we are better off not wasting more time than we need to on our physical appearance. We look in the mirror, and we see ourselves—bed head, unshaven, in need of a haircut, whatever. But that's what we see. We don't have the same outer physical struggles that girls do. Or at least we don't focus on them to the same extent.

Stop Looking in Other People's Mirrors

Hey . . . cut it out! Stop doing that. You need to look in *your* mirror, not hers. Who you are on the inside is really much more important than what you see on the outside. Believe it. You may not *feel* like it's true, but it is. Every girl is made exactly the way she is for the perfect reason that God intended.

There is nothing more attractive to a guy than a girl who feels comfortable in her own skin. If this is *not* the impression you're getting from the guys you're hanging out with, the odds are that you're surrounded by the wrong people.

I know. You're probably thinking it's unrealistic to say, "I am perfect just the way I am, flaws and all!" Well, say it until you believe it anyway. Practice it. It is only when you start to grasp this concept that you will begin to understand real beauty, the kind of beauty that God created and intended for you to have. Even if it's not something you feel, it's something you can *know*.

It's amazing to see how often girls compare themselves to others, from their height and weight to their hair color, complexion, and shoe size. **When you look at the girl's mirror next to yours, you'll always be looking at a slant . . . so STOP!** You can't see things for what they truly are when you're looking at an angle. Things never look like they really are.

Guys like to be around girls who know they are valuable. Being secure is a *very* attractive quality. Guys appreciate a girl who knows her worth because then *we* can value it. It sets the standard for us. If a guy sees that a girl knows how she wants to be treated, then he usually treats her that way. If she expects a guy to be kind and loving, he will do that too. If he doesn't treat her well, she wants nothing to do with him.

In fact, when a girl doesn't feel good about herself, she can in subtle ways put pressure on a guy and expect him to solve this problem for her. That drives a guy crazy, and he runs as far away from that girl as he can get!

NEWS FLASH!

What you see is what guys will see, and that's the truth.

When you know you are valued because God values you, then you become more attractive to a guy. The trick is whether or not you can accept this truth about yourself. If you do, and you can embrace it, so will guys. Otherwise, how does a guy know how he's supposed to do it?

The good news is, it's all in your hands. It's up to you to decide your worth—not the magazines, TV shows, popularity contests, your friends, or even your parents! You have to choose to see that you are valuable before anybody else is going to. (Notice I said it's a choice. Regardless of how you feel, you have to get your mind involved!)

GUY TIP:

A guy knows pretty fast when he meets a girl if she thinks she is valuable and knows she's special and important. (We're not talking about being arrogant here.) The more special you know you are, the more special you become to a guy.

> To dream of the person you
> would like to be is to waste the
> person you are.
>
> —Anonymous

Your Body . . . the Perfect Body

The perfect body is not the one you see on TV. It's not the airbrushed version of a supermodel on a magazine cover. It's not six feet tall and 102 pounds with an oversized chest and a tiny waist. And this is no pep talk—it's the truth. The sooner you stop accepting the lie being handed to you every day, the quicker you will move toward attaining real beauty.

The perfect body does not jog around in slow motion on the beach all day and stop to pose in the wind so her hair can blow gently in the breeze. Even guys know this much. We may be fascinated by images like these, but we know they are not part of the real world.

The perfect body is not what you see in the mirror; it's the one you are in. **When you learn to love your body, it will love you back.**

The perfect body is imperfect. There is no one single body that will be viewed as "perfect" by ten different guys. But that's okay. Why? Because you weren't created to be perfect for ten different guys—you were created to be perfect for your heavenly Father and also perhaps for the one special guy he has handpicked for you.

There's an old song that says, "God made you something special. You're the only one of your kind." That is the truth about you. God made you exactly the way he intended. Did you ever stop to think that God made you in a way that is completely unique and special? There is no one just like you. There never has been, and there never will be. You're the only you. And your friends—girls and guys—and perhaps someday your husband, will be so happy they got to know *you*.

> You must love yourself before you love another. By accepting yourself and fully being what you are . . . your simple presence can make others happy.
>
> —Jane Roberts

So don't insult God. He made you, and he knows what he is doing.

Turn off the TV. Stop gazing at celebrities. Love yourself. Look in the mirror and laugh at your imperfections and say, "That's goofy, but I can accept it and even like it, because I know God made me this way!" Then toss those dumb airbrushed magazines with articles on how to do four hundred sit-ups and have the "perfect body" and say, "Thanks, I needed a good laugh."

TOTALLY TREASURED

Love yourself, and put more effort into your heart than any other part of you. Then you can see yourself for who you really are—nothing more, and nothing less. You are God's perfect and unique design.

NEWS FLASH!

The average girl weighs 144 pounds and is a size 12. This is healthy.[2]

Studies found that three minutes spent looking at a fashion magazine caused 70 percent of girls to feel depressed, less attractive, guilty, and ashamed.[4]

Eighty percent of ten-year-olds have dieted.[3]

One out of four girls suffers from an eating disorder.[5]

Half of girls, by their first year through college, will have an incurable form of HPV or genital herpes.[6]

The weight-loss industry brings in forty billion dollars a year convincing you that you aren't good enough the way you are.[7]

The average teen girl sees four to six hundred advertisements per day. About one-third of these have a direct message about being beautiful.[8]

About half of teen girls who are sexually active have sexually transmitted diseases.[9]

In a study of eleven- to seventeen-year-old girls, the number one wish was to be thinner.[10]

You know that you are supposed to like yourself, but you're being told every day that you need to be more beautiful. This is crazy . . .

Can You Separate Fantasy from Reality?

Fantasy: You can and should diet and exercise your way to looking like a model, and you have failed somehow if you don't make it.

Fact: Everyone is born with a different body. No one body type is better or worse than another. Models usually have the type of genes that allows them to be very tall and thin. Very few people acutally look like that.

Fantasy: Boys only like very thin girls.

Fact: Teenage boys may like to look at very thin, pretty girls, but they often prefer to date regular-looking girls who aren't intimidating to them.

Fantasy: Celebrities naturally look fabulous.

Fact: Most celebrities spend hours a day polishing their "look," and they sacrifice a lot to get there. What's more, very, very few actors actually "make it." Most go on to do other things long before they get anywhere near prime-time TV or the movies.

These are common messages that girls hear every day and are often distorted between fantasy and fact. Be sure you know the facts!

Fantasy: You have to look, dress, and eat like your friends or you won't be accepted.

Fact: Everyone has a different body type, and you have to take care of your body in a way that feels comfortable and flattering to you. Being healthy is important, but having friends who accept you for who you are is the ultimate goal. If your friends are pressuring you to be their mirror image, you probably have unhealthy friendships.

5

Miss Magnet

A girl ran into the store to pick up a few items. She headed for the express line, where the clerk was talking on the phone with his back turned to her.

"Excuse me," she said, "I'm in a hurry. Could you check me out, please?"

The clerk turned, looked at her for a moment, smiled, and said, "Not bad." ■

Attraction

You're always sending out signals, giving messages, or interacting with guys, whether you realize it or not. There's nothing you can do about it. The real question is, do you know what types of signals and messages you are sending? Every girl has her own unique force field that can have either a negative or a positive pull toward its center. Which one is yours?

Guess what? Girls are a lot like magnets. Here are three facts about magnets and girls:

- Magnets attract magnetic materials.
  - Girls attract guys.
- Magnets act at a distance.
  - Guys have always found girls, wherever they are.
- Every magnet is positively or negatively charged.
  - Every girl has a positive or a negative attraction.

A lot of girls put a ton of effort into attracting guys. But that's not necessary. **Most girls don't realize that you are trying to create something you already have.**

You were born with an attraction. It won't leave you. Your job is to be sure the attraction in you will have a positive pull. The pictures of movie stars and fashion models are not real; they are styled and airbrushed to create desire. Girls see images of these impossibly beautiful women and desire to look just like them; guys see these women and desire *them*!

Turns out, this is a desire that can never be satisfied. It's as if someone is saying, "I know you're thirsty. Have a drink of water." Then they hand you a glass of water from the ocean. Your thirst cannot be quenched with saltwater.

Your desire to feel beautiful does not come solely from looking beautiful. It has to come from somewhere else. You have to realize that you are already attractive to guys. You don't have to reinvent the wheel. Okay, so maybe you're not attractive to every guy on the planet. Who cares? Why would you want to be? It's not realistic.

God created you in his image. That's right! It's amazing, wonderful, and mind-blowing. You are God's manifestation of beauty to guys *already*. Guys have wanted girls since the history of history. We are pulled toward you because you are a magnet to us.

So which one do you have: a positive attraction or a negative one? The question isn't if guys will be attracted to you, but what type of guys you will attract.

Guys Don't Have a Clue

"Why are guys jerks?"

"Why doesn't he love me anymore?"

"Why do I attract guys who treat me so crummy?"

"Why does he just want to be physical?"

"Why can't I trust him?"

Do questions like these sound familiar? I hear girls saying stuff like this all the time! You seem so frustrated with the results you are getting for the effort you are putting into your relationships. There are good reasons for this.

Today's culture doesn't promote respectable guys. Instead, it gives messages to us that say, "You're captain of the stud ship if you can land a ton of chicks. Do your push-ups, build your abs, don't show your feelings, and make tons of money.

Oh, and being with a hot girl means you'll be hot too." This is confusing stuff for guys, and it makes our relationships harder.

WARNING!

A guy may want to do the right things, but he may just have some really bad habits. Many teenage guys don't realize that they're being selfish, hurtful, disrespectful, sarcastic, and unromantic. Keep in mind, these aren't excuses, just explanations. Guys are usually thinking about themselves a lot more than they are thinking about you at this age.

There are lots of guys out there. There are guys who think it's amazing if they burp for fifteen seconds. There are guys who think it's a hoot to eat food off your plate without asking. There are guys who think they're so special because they have every varsity letter available, which may actually be a really special thing to do—except when they flaunt it every chance they get.

Let's face it, teenage guys are not the guys you see in the movies. They have a long way to go in the "get a clue" department.

In order to have strong muscles, you have to build them. You have to exercise them and work for them. We're talking about the most important muscle in your body—your heart. Be careful with it. It's much better to have it unbroken than to have to rebuild it from scratch.

If you provide a *positive* attraction, a guy will want to know you for who you are. He will work to make you feel special, he will build your trust by being truthful, and he will encourage you to be everything you were created to be.

If you provide a *negative* attraction, a guy will try to get something from you. He will tell you whatever you want to hear in order to get what he wants. This may be as simple as attention or as serious as sex. Even if a guy really wants another girl, sometimes he's willing to take what he can get and settles for a girl who gives off a clear signal that she's all too available.

Sending out a positive attraction to guys won't be easy. It may seem as though you are swimming upstream against the current. Sometimes you'll feel like you just want to quit and give in to the pressure. Doing what's right, good, and healthy is almost never easy. It usually goes against what everyone else is doing. It can be really, really hard. But it's worth it.

You know what else? You're worth it too.

6

Treasure or Target?

Two girls walked into a pizza joint, anxiously awaiting their dates for the evening. One girl was dressed in a low-cut silk shirt and blue jeans that barely covered her hips. Her nails were polished, her hair was beautifully styled, and her makeup was applied to perfection. The other girl wore an oversized white sweatshirt and a pair of sweatpants. Her hair was in a ponytail, and she hadn't had time to do much else to her appearance before rushing over to the restaurant after volleyball practice.

The guys showed up, and both couples sat down to talk while they waited for their pizza. The girl in the silk shirt clung to her date. She ran her fingers through his hair, blew him kisses, and giggled throughout the meal. The other girl kept her physical distance from her date. She was just eager to get to know him, so they had a fun conversation.

At the end of the evening, the girl in the silk shirt was persuaded to go with her date to good ol' Lookout Mountain. The other girl suggested to her date that they play some pool before she had to leave to meet her curfew. ∎

The Great Treasure Hunt

The way you dress, the way you act, and even your attitude play important roles in the way that guys see you. It's only natural, then, that the way guys see you is in direct relation to the way guys treat you. The way guys treat you can affect your future relationships.

Imagine something valuable, something worth grabbing hold of and simply admiring. Does that describe you? Or would you be better described as someone a guy can take from in order to feel better about himself? Just ask yourself this question: **"When people look at me, do they see me as a 'treasure,' or do they see me as a 'target'?"**

It's not a complicated question. Think about when you're spending time with your friends on Saturday night, walking around the mall, going to the movies, or hanging out at your local chill spot. Put yourself in whatever normal, everyday circumstances are common to you. Do you feel like those people see you as a treasure? Or do they see you as a target?

Keep in mind that the important thing here isn't really the way *you* see yourself in these situations, but the way other people do. Sometimes you've gotta step out of your own shoes and into the shoes of other people in order to see how you're coming across to them.

Most girls would love to have guys look at them as though they were as valuable as gold—an absolute treasure. I mean, think about it. Treasures are things people value more than anything else. Treasures are cherished, adored, and appreciated. And guess what? Guys are searching for a special treasure! We are longing to find that one perfect gem God has chosen as a perfect match, just for us.

On the other hand, in today's culture, plenty of people

are looking for a good target. You know what I mean—another trophy on a guy's shelf that he can brag about to his buddies so they'll think he's smooth or tough for having "gotten that prize." Maybe you think that's a little extreme, but you're a girl. You don't know what guys are like when we want to look cool in front of others. The stakes can be pretty high for a guy playing the game of "cool."

These guys aren't as interested in a treasure hunt. They are often satisfied with whatever is easily available.

HERE'S A SECRET:

What impression do you give to others when you meet them? When you hang out with them? When you date them? Are you a treasure or a target? If you aren't seen as one, you're probably being seen as the other.

A Girl's Value Menu

If you could choose to be either of the following hypothetical girls, which one would you prefer?

GIRL A: When a guy looks at you, he thinks most guys don't have a chance. Not because you are too beautiful or because you're mean, but because you don't seem interested in *all* boys. A guy sees you and knows it is going to take a lot of effort to develop a friendship with you. He's going to have to use his heart and his head if he's going to have a chance at any type of relationship with you. When a guy makes an effort to meet you, he stares into your eyes as though he is trying to see right into your heart. He's there to help you, not harm you. He wants you to know you are really important and he wants the best for you. He compliments you for no reason at all, and he doesn't require something of you at the end of the sentence . . . or the evening. He looks out for you, even when you aren't looking out for yourself. A guy who spends time with you wants to make you laugh and smile. Seeing you giggle when he looks at you makes him happier than most anything. He simply wants you to know you are wonderful, beautiful, and deserve nothing but the best, with no strings attached. And he doesn't want anything in return for this at all.

GIRL B: A guy looks at you and thinks you are a mighty fine piece of meat. He thinks you look like someone that he can try some new stuff with. He knows he doesn't have to marry you in order to get you to do whatever he wants. He's determined to win you over tonight—and by "win," he's only thinking of his own satisfaction and pleasure. He doesn't really care about meeting your needs—especially not in the long run—as long as you can meet his. He wants something from you, and he figures that with minimal effort you'll probably give it to him.

You may think those two examples are pretty extreme and fairly radical. You're right. You may even be thinking, *Yeah, right, if a guy does exist for Girl A, he doesn't live on this planet!* Or maybe you're just thinking people aren't as black or white as either of the examples provided.

Drum roll: here comes the point. Just about every girl imaginable would pick A over B. And believe it or not, guys love friendships and relationships, with Girl A! The thing to note here is that *you* are the person who determines which girl you are seen as. Let me say that again. It's not up to anyone else to make that decision—it's up to YOU!

Write Your Own Instructions

A girl who displays her sex appeal, a party girl, or a loud-mouthed, insecure girl who is craving a guy's attention all the time likely isn't going to be swept off her feet by a handsome prince who just wants to stare into her eyes all day. Not that you just want to be stared at, but you get the point.

Likewise, a girl who doesn't use her body in sexual ways to get attention, one who cares about her reputation and has goals and relationship standards ahead of time, is not going to settle for anything less than someone who cares for her. She refuses to be seen as a target, so guys don't look at her and think that she is prey. She has those rules written all over her.

Guys see the instructions for girls ahead of time— before we get within twenty feet of them—so we know if we want to start out on their terms or not. Every girl may *want* to be seen as valuable, precious, and as someone to be treasured. **But in reality, many girls who want to be treasures actually look more like targets; they just can't figure out why!**

Well, hello! Girls like this try so hard to please a guy by putting forth a ton of effort, only to get heartache in return. They wind up making comments like, "Why did he say he loved me?" "Why are all guys such jerks?" and "Guys will do or say anything to get sex." That's the hurt talking, the experience of betrayal and pain. What they're really saying is, "Why doesn't that person care about me or think I am valuable?"

> Though we travel the world over to find the beautiful, we must carry it with us or find it not.
>
> —Ralph Waldo Emerson

GUY TIP:

I know this may sting a bit, but the decision about how guys see you is yours. How you are seen is up to you, NOT US! It is up to you and you alone. If you know you are valuable, then more guys will see you as a treasure. Notice that I didn't say if you *think* you are valuable. You have to *know* it. You have to own it. You have to live it.

It's What We Don't See . . .

If you show a guy everything and tell him everything there is to show and tell right up front, it becomes obvious that you're an easy catch and probably available to any guy, just for the asking. Guys like to discover things, so you have to let them discover you. I realize that's probably hard sometimes, because you desire to be known. You want guys to know all about you—the real you. I get that. But the fact is, you can stay real to who you are without giving it all away up front.

If a guy learns too much about you—your secrets, hopes, dreams, fears, and feelings—he doesn't have much left to wonder about, and he becomes less interested. Remember, he wants to find a treasure, and a treasure isn't left out on the beach for everyone to find. A treasure is hidden. A guy has to search for it, map it out, chart the territory, dig for it, and finally discover it. Only after that journey can he appreciate the treasure for what it is.

Ruff, Ruff!

Dogs like to chase things. So do guys. Today, many people say, "Times are different." They think it's okay for girls to chase guys and ask them out because it's an equal playing field. Honestly, that's just not the way guys are best wired.

If you flirt with guys and go after them, you may wind up making them feel good about themselves without them having to do anything. It may boost a guy's ego. They may even be really interested in you, because you're making things so easy for them. Eventually, though, many guys will lose interest in this game because it just isn't challenging. It's not exciting, enticing, or captivating.

Don't get me wrong. You should always be yourself—the amazing person God made you. I just want you to understand that a girl who is mysterious is more attractive. Another benefit is that you don't waste your time pouring everything in to guys who aren't meant for you. **Maintaining a bit of**

mystery is a way of protecting your heart. A treasure isn't meant for everyone, just the one who has taken the time and done the work to discover it.

Take Your Heart Off Your Sleeve

Reach over and take your heart off your sleeve and put it back inside where it will be protected. That's where your heart belongs, not outside for everyone to see how it can get beaten up and abused. If you're a drama queen, knock it off. It's unattractive.

Your heart is for God, for yourself, and to be shared with others carefully. It is your wellspring of life—not a Friday night trinket. Your heart, oddly enough, is your most important physical and spiritual feature. Remember, your heart is important because it is the key to being vulnerable and real.

> To wear your heart on your sleeve isn't a very good plan; you should wear it inside, where it functions best.
>
> —Margaret Thatcher

The Bible talks more about the heart than any other part of the body. We are told to guard our heart. There is no mystery in a girl who boldly says everything she thinks, feels, and experiences the first few times guys meet her.

Lots of girls simply toss their hearts out there for the taking. They yell, scream, cry, and are overly dramatic in public. They're usually very happy or terribly upset. When it comes to guys, they are in an emotional heaven or hell. They wear their insides on their outsides. To a guy, this is very unattractive.

TOTALLY TREASURED

Remember: you have a heart perfectly designed for you by the greatest of designers. Your heart is there for you to take care of, so when you expose it, it will be cherished and taken care of in return.

Allow your heart to be so wrapped up in God that a guy has to ask for directions to get to it.

7

Who's Your Daddy?

Before I made you in your mother's womb,
I chose you. Before you were born,
I set you apart.

—Jeremiah 1:5

A man came home one evening after a rough day at the office. He was trying to read the newspaper, but his children constantly interrupted him. One child came and asked for money so she could buy ice cream. So he reached into his pocket and gave his daughter the needed coins.

Another child came to him in tears. He had hurt his leg and wanted his daddy to kiss the hurt away.

His eldest son came to him with an algebra problem. Eventually, he was able to help his son find the right answer.

Finally, his youngest child burst into the room looking for good old Dad. "What do *you* want?" he asked, exasperated.

The youngster snuggled up close to her father and said, "Oh, Daddy, I don't want anything. I just want to sit on your lap!" ■

A Father's Love

You may have the most wonderful dad in the whole world, or you may have never even met him. No matter your own experiences with your father, you can read this story and smile.

Every child is different. All of us have our own likes and dislikes. Each personality is defined by different strengths, dreams, and even quirks. Yet at the end of the day, as different as we are in many ways, we are really the same. Each of us wants to be loved by our parents.

> My dad told me when I went to high school, "It's not what you do when you walk in the door that matters. It's what you do when you walk out." That's when you've made a lasting impression.
>
> —Jim Thorne

I don't have a lot of memories of my childhood. Most of it wasn't something that I want to remember. We moved away from Florida when I was around seven years old. I remember hearing something about the word *divorce*, and it involved Mom and Dad. I wasn't sure exactly what that meant, but I knew it wasn't good, and things were going to be different somehow. It made me angry, but as a kid I didn't know why. I still got to see my dad on holidays and during the summers. He'd come to visit occasionally, but we moved pretty far away. I guess it was hard on everyone.

Although my brain has blocked out most of my childhood memories, there are some that will never go away. Most are about my dad. I remember the aboveground pool we had and how my sister and I would ride around on his back while he swam. I felt like I was gliding above the water as if riding on a dolphin. He'd tell us the story of the "Three Little Pigs" and do the wolf's voice by mumbling on top of the water. My sister and I would listen in pure amazement.

When my dad got home from work and parked his car in the driveway, I'd stop whatever I was doing, which usually involved dirt, a stick, and insects. I'd run and jump into his arms from three feet away! There was something about my dad's embrace and smell and the feel of his strong arms that made everything in the world much better. I guess sometimes we don't need an explanation about how much we're loved. We just need to be hugged.

I used to do this acrobatic trick that I'm fairly sure is plugged into everybody's DNA, because all kids somehow know how to do it. I'd grab my dad's thumbs, and with all my might, I'd kick my way up his legs and onto his chest like I was climbing a mountain. Then, when I got to the top, I'd heave myself backward into a perfect flip and land on my feet. Of course, I knew it wouldn't matter how I landed, because my dad's arms always found a way to keep me upright.

Maybe this chapter should have been first. Maybe it should have been the entire book, because something has become painfully obvious to me. After talking to teens for years and reading, writing, researching, and observing them, I realized we're all looking for fatherly love.

When we aren't loved correctly as children, it usually spills out in our lives, making a mess of us. It translates into our self-worth, our self-image, our friendships, our jobs, our relationships, and our marriages. And in girls, especially, it becomes obvious that things are not as simple as they seem.

My Two Dads

This may be the single most important thing I know to tell you: **you have two fathers, and there isn't a guy you will meet who can be either of them.** First, you have a biological dad. (Even if for some unfortunate reason you don't know him, you still have one.) No guy can be your dad and replace what you need from him. Other guys don't know how to, nor do they want to.

> God walks with us. . . . He scoops us up in his arms or simply sits with us in silent strength until we cannot avoid that awesome recognition that yes, even now, he is here.
>
> —Gloria Gaither

You will not be able to love yourself until you know you are loved by your father. Now don't panic. This is good news. The dad you were born with may have failed in his fatherly role. (Even the best fathers aren't perfect.) There's an amazing backup plan for those of you who may not have experienced the best, or even adequate, fathering.

Second, in addition to our earthly father, we all have a heavenly Father. Most people today don't equate fatherly love with God. But the good news is, *God is your Father.* He loves you. He is there for you. And he never gets tired of your wanting to grab his hands and do backflips. It doesn't matter what you've been through or who you are, where you've been or where you're going. Your Father in heaven isn't going anywhere.

One thing I like to tell teens when we're talking about God is, "You have to know not only *who* you are, but more important, *whose* you are." If you can't embrace that, you will always be trying to fill a void. Many girls, and perhaps even you, try so hard to find worth, beauty, and confidence in your relationships. Then you are disappointed when your efforts fail. It's like putting a quarter in the bubblegum machine, and the only thing that comes out is a handful of dirt. Side note: dirt is not good for chewing. I've tried it. After all, I am a guy.

WARNING!

The guy you are dating (or want to date) *cannot* make you complete. If you think he will, you will become disheartened. Guys cannot create a girl's beauty. Guys can't create a girl's worth. So if you are searching for fulfillment in a guy, he will always fail and disappoint you. He will always fall short of your expectations.

You Are Beautiful

Girls are usually searching for something. You may be searching for beauty, cute clothes, makeup, the right body, and the perfect guy to go with it all. But beauty can only come from one place. It doesn't come from a clothes store, and it certainly doesn't come from a guy. Beauty comes from your heavenly Father. **It's up to you to see yourself as beautiful.** If you want someone else to find you beautiful, this is not an option.

Every girl has a moment in her life that's tragic. Maybe it's the first time someone called you ugly, the first time someone took advantage of you, the first time you were neglected, the first time you needed someone and no one was there, or the first time you thought you weren't good enough.

As has been often said, the greatest trick the devil ever pulled was convincing the world he didn't exist. Boy is that true! In a book by John Eldredge, he carefully points out, "You cannot win a battle that you will not admit you are in."[1] And probably one of the best tactics the devil ever used on you was convincing you that you weren't okay just the way you are. Oh, he's recruited all sorts of help—cosmetics companies, the fashion industry, MTV; they all tell you the same thing: "Sure, you're beautiful! But you can be so much more beautiful for just $9.99." Translation: you aren't so beautiful after all.

> The beginning of anxiety is the end of faith, and the beginning of true faith is the end of anxiety.
>
> —George Mueller

If you're like most girls, you are constantly fighting the idea that you're too big, too small, too round, too thin, too pale, too freckled, too smart, not sexy enough, and definitely not as good as *her*. That's not what your Father is telling you, but are you listening to him? He's telling you that you are not broken; that nothing is too big, too small, too round, too thin, too pale, too freckled, too smart, or not sexy enough about you; and that you're definitely just as good as *her*! Your Father wants you to listen to him, sit on his lap, and spend time in his presence. When you do that, you'll find the image you're so desperately searching for.

GUY TIP:

The best guy in the world cannot give you every-thing you need. He can't be perfect. He can't fill your voids. Most important, none of that is his job. A guy doesn't want a girl who needs him to be her dad. A guy doesn't want to convince you that you are beautiful. He wants to sit in admiration of your beauty! But he can't do that unless you let him. And you can't let him until you believe it yourself.

Never Alone

What would it be like if you didn't worry? Really, what would your life look like? What if, no matter what your circumstances, you believed:

- We don't have to worry, because God has a plan better than our own (Matthew 6:25–27).
- God hears our fervent prayers (James 5:16).
- God knows us more intimately than we know ourselves (Psalm 139:13).
- God cares about our deepest desires (Psalm 37:4).
- God has sympathy for how fragile we are (Hebrews 4:15).
- God longs to be gracious to us (Isaiah 30:18).
- God is happy to give us an entire kingdom (Luke 12:32).

If you could honestly look to your Father for all of these things, you wouldn't worry so much about high school or boyfriends or making out. Think about the guys you know.

Then read the list again. Don't guys seem lacking if you believe all of those things? You may just realize that guys are fairly limited in what we can do for you. We don't make things; we complete the things God has made. That includes caring for you.

Go ahead, read the list one more time. When you realize you can believe those things, you may even start to grasp the concept Isaiah talked about when he said:

> *The people who trust the LORD will become strong again. They will rise up as an eagle in the sky; they will run and not need rest; they will walk and not become tired.*
> —Isaiah 40:31

OFF THE RECORD:

You have to tell guys who you are and show us what you're worth. You can't expect us to tell you. We don't have the right to do that, and besides, we'll always foul it up.

Into the Fire

Think about the hurts in your life: your fears, your failures, your disappointments, and your heartaches. Write them down on a sheet of paper. Then let your heavenly Father take your hand and help you throw them into the fire. You don't have to keep holding on to them. God has some awesome hugs just waiting for you, and you can do as many climbing backflips as you want!

Because God has
made us for
himself, our hearts
are restless until
they rest in him.

—Saint Augustine

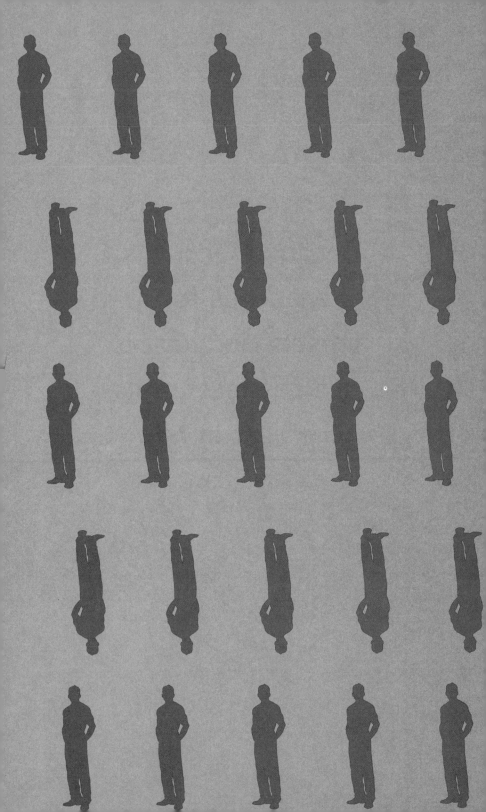

1　（2）　3　4

Guys Are Waffles

*The L*ORD *has told you, human,*
what is good; he has told you
what he wants from you: to do
what is right to other people,
love being kind to others,
and live humbly,
obeying your God.

—Micah 6:8

8

The Five Toughest Questions Girls Ask
(And How to Answer Them)

GIRL HAIRCUTS

Susie: Oh! You got a haircut! It's so cute!

Laura: Really? Do you think so? I wasn't so sure when she gave me the mirror. You don't think it's too fluffy looking?

Susie: No way! It's perfect. I'd love to get my hair cut like that, but my face is too wide. I'm stuck with this stuff. It doesn't do a thing.

Laura: Are you serious? Your face is so adorable. You could easily get it layered—that would make you look so pretty. I was actually going to do that, except I was afraid it would make my neck look longer than it is already.

Susie: Come on, Laura. I'd love to have your neck! Anything to take attention away from this two-by-four frame I've got. ▼

Laura: Are you kidding? Girls would kill to have your shoulders. Your clothes just flow on your beautiful body. Just look at my arms—see how short they are? If I had your shoulders, I could get clothes to fit me so much easier.

GUY HAIRCUTS
Dave: Haircut?
Sean: Yeah. ■

Waffle Boy

Have you ever noticed that guys say things that are . . . uh, simple? It's true. Our conversations, our behavior, and our brains differ greatly from yours. It's not because guys are simple creatures. Actually, we are complex, fascinating, and just as interesting, yet different.

The fact is, girls have very different brains than guys. If your brain is like a jumbled-up plate of spaghetti, you could call a guy—Waffle Boy![1]

Girls, please understand that guys are simply different than you are, and there is nothing you can do to change that. Consider the "logical" process that occurs in a guy's mind when he is asked five very simple, yet confusing, questions by a member of the female species:

- What are you thinking?
- Do you love me?
- Do I look too heavy in this outfit?

- Do you think she is prettier than I am?
- What would you do if I died?

WARNING!

Each of these questions is guaranteed to explode into a major fight if the guy doesn't answer it properly—which is to say, it's going to be awkward for him. Let's take a look.

WHAT ARE YOU THINKING?

The correct answer to this question, of course, is, "I'm sorry if I've been preoccupied. I was just thinking about what a warm, wonderful, and beautiful girl you are and what a lucky guy I am to have met you."

Obviously, this statement bears no resemblance whatsoever to what the guy was really thinking at the time. Most likely he was thinking about one of these things:

a. Baseball.
b. Football.
c. How good cheese puffs would taste right now.
d. Who is winning in a game of Madden?
e. Will she be mad if I burp right now?

DO YOU LOVE ME?

The correct answer to this question is, "Yes." If any guy feels the need to elaborate, he may answer, "Yes, of course!"

Wrong answers include:

a. I suppose so.
b. Would it make you feel better if I said yes?
c. That depends on what you mean by "love."
d. Does it matter?
e. Who, me?

DO I LOOK TOO HEAVY IN THIS OUTFIT?

The correct male response to this question is a confident and emphatic, "No, of course not," followed by quickly leaving the room.

Wrong answers include:

a. I wouldn't say you look heavy, but I wouldn't call you thin either.
b. Compared to what?
c. A little extra weight looks good on you.
d. Lots of people look heavier than you.
e. Could you repeat the question?

DO YOU THINK SHE'S PRETTIER THAN I AM?

The "she" in the question could be anyone. It could be an ex-girlfriend, a pretty girl passing by whom the guy was staring at so hard he almost caused a traffic accident, or an actress in a movie you both just saw. In any case, the correct response is, without any doubt, "No, you are much prettier."

Wrong answers include:
a. Not prettier, just pretty in a different way.
b. I don't know how anyone goes about rating such things.
c. Yes, but you have a better personality.
d. Only in the sense that she's taller and thinner.
e. Could you repeat the question?

WHAT WOULD YOU DO IF I DIED?

Correct answer: "My love, in the event of your untimely demise, life would cease to have meaning for me. If that happened, I would hurl myself under the tires of the first delivery truck that came my way."

Wrong answers include:
a. I'd cry.
b. I'd give you the best funeral you could ever wish for!
c. You'll never die.
d. I don't ever want to think about that.
e. What kind of question is *that*?

Here's the point: guys would be much more comfortable if we just had specific guidelines for understanding and dealing with girls. But because this stuff can't be completely formulated, we wind up frustrated, confused, and sometimes just plain baffled.

When you ask those questions, or similar ones, you're usually looking for something far greater than the face value of the question (as if that weren't enough). You are looking for affirmations that you are valuable—the very stuff you can't find from someone other than yourself.

Inside of our great guy and girl designs, God gave us very different brains. The girls got all the spaghetti-ish, chatty, love babies, great eye contact, and a thousand other girl-thing brains. Guys got the compartmentalized, one at a time is better, get to the point, let's just blow it up, guy-thing brains. We're just different.

Once you understand the differences, it will make your life a lot easier. If you want to understand how guys are wired, first you'll have to step outside of your own skin and try—just try—to look at things through different eyes.

Mixing these two ways of thinking about the world together in harmony is what eventually makes for a pretty balanced marriage. But for now, how do you handle it? Well, c'mon with me and take a look into the goofy heads of guys and see what you think . . .

May I Have a Waffle?

First of all, guys don't think everything has to be connected to everything else. We don't think about girls all the time. Girls don't even cross our minds when we're out on the field at football practice or playing paintball with our friends.

We are in the moment. When you see us playing video games (which we probably do way too much), we're just playing video games. We aren't thinking about homework, our dog, washing our clothes, whether or not we smell, or you. We are simply playing the game.

A guy's brain has a lot of compartments. Each one is separated from the others. They even have dividers. Guys are free to come and go into each compartment at will. But these compartments don't spend time together, and they don't usually invite each other over just to talk and spend time together.

When guys spend a lot of time in one compartment, we get good at whatever that compartment involves. It may be sports, being cool, learning math, flirting, whatever. We focus on what we're good at and ignore the other stuff. Guys don't look in the mirror and dwell on one tiny blemish. We tend to look at the one good aspect of ourselves and then build everything else around that. A lot of guys find our identity in what we're good at doing; it becomes our calling card.

In the middle of a phone conversation, guys will often wonder, *What is the point of this conversation? What do I need to do?* Whereas girls usually think, *Why does there have to be a point? Why can't we just talk?* It's because our brains are different.

So which one is better: the waffle or the spaghetti? I ask teens that question all the time. The guys very quickly respond, "Guys! Dudes rule!" The girls, thankfully, have another response. You think about it for a second, then you usually say, "Neither one is better than the other." That's because girls tend to be a bit more fair by nature. And you are right. The answer really is, "Neither." Guys and girls are just different.

9

What We Don't Say

True eloquence consists of saying all
that should be said, and that only.

—François de La Rochefoucauld

Donnie was trying to prove to his girlfriend that
girls talk more than guys. "Look, Emily, here's a study
that shows that guys, on average, use only fifteen
thousand words a day."

"So?" she said. But she was actually curious to
hear the remainder of the study results.

"It also shows that girls, on average, use thirty thousand words a day!" Donnie pronounced triumphantly.

Emily thought about this for a moment and said,
"I'm sure that's the case. After all, girls use twice as
many words, because they have to repeat everything
they say."

"What?" Donnie asked. ■

Something to Talk About

Girls generally use more words to express yourselves. For one thing, your vocabularies are more advanced, and you know a lot more about expressing your feelings. Think about it. As we saw back in chapter 3, guys will usually say, "I think . . ." about something. Girls, on the other hand, will talk about the very same thing, but say, "I feel . . ."

I have to admit, there are some parts of guys' brains where there just isn't much going on, but that's okay! Those are the calm, nonverbal, undisturbed portions that we retreat to. These involve TV, video games, or just sitting around staring at the wall. Guys also have lots of ideas and experiences that we think about but just don't want to verbalize. That doesn't mean we can't experience them.

> After dinner, Christie told her boyfriend Mike, "Last night I dreamed that you gave me a diamond necklace for Valentine's Day. What do you think it means?"
> "You'll know by tomorrow night," he said. The next night, Mike came over to Christie's with a package and gave it to her. Delighted, she opened it and found a book entitled *The Meaning of Dreams*.

Guys don't need to talk, vent, hug one another, and cry. We just need to sit and be a part of something else.

How Brains Work

There was a study done by a woman named Leah Ariniello from the Society of Neuroscience called "Gender and the Brain".[1] I thought it was pretty cool. She mapped the brains of an equal number of guys and girls as they tried to get out of a 3-D virtual maze. On average, the guys got out fifty-four seconds faster than the girls.

Why? Because guys used the part of their brains that relied on geometry, and girls depended on memorizing landmarks along the way. This is one of the only things I'll boast about as a guy—maybe we can get out of mazes faster! Okay, sometimes you just have to let us have our "moment." LOL, laugh out loud, or whatever that means . . . it's a joke!

Girls are often better at memorizing things than guys are. You can memorize more words than we can and associate them with other things better than we can.

Your brain is more protective of itself and more aware of what may be harmful or negative to you. That's probably why guys jump out of windows onto trees, skateboard off twenty-foot concrete drop-offs, and make little bombs that nearly blow our arms off, all in the name of a good laugh or great adventure. Girls just look at us and say, "You guys are dumb. That's dangerous." Guess what? You're usually right. And we usually don't realize it until we're on the ground holding a broken ankle, and our friends are laughing at us.

It's the experience, rather than the logic, that tells guys that having bottle-rocket wars with one another isn't the smartest thing to do with our time. It's only after the bottle rocket whizzes by our face, hits us in the eyeball, and we feel how much it hurts that we realize it was a pretty dumb thing to do.

Here are more interesting things about guys and girls:

- Most little boys are concerned with dominance and are rewarded for being the boss, whether in Little League or on the corner selling lemonade.

- Seventy-five to 93 percent of interruptions in conversation are made by guys.[2]

- Most guys think that becoming a girl would be more restricting.

- Within relationships, girls tend to resolve the day-to-day issues, and guys usually prefer to settle the huge disputes.

- Guys often overestimate their intelligence, and girls tend to underestimate theirs. (Hard to believe, I know.)

- Girls are less likely to be caught and ticketed for speeding than guys.[3]

- When guys perform well at something, they tend to attribute their success to their own skill and intelligence. If they perform badly, they tend to blame it on bad luck or some other factor beyond their control.[4]

- Little girls in groups usually learn to blend in, to be sensitive to one another's feelings, to avoid boasting, and to believe they're punished by exclusion when they are bossy.

- Guys overwhelmingly believe that it's harder to be a guy today than it was twenty years ago.[5]

- Guys think that greeting other guys in the hallway with a punch is acceptable.

Do Us a Favor

If you want to understand guys better, talk to us in a way that allows us to focus on one thing at a time. If you want to talk about how we feel, ask us direct, open-ended questions. Don't try to read something into what we are trying to say.

Since guys are generally more direct and use fewer analogies and touchy-feely words, what we say is probably exactly what we're thinking.

> **GUY TIP:**
>
> Give guys one task at a time, and we will be more likely to focus on it and do a better job. Trying to think, act, or talk like a girl is uncomfortable for guys, and we aren't likely to be good at it. Two words about guys' words: *face value.*

Parallel Play

Research done on how kids play gave birth to the idea of "parallel play," which is all about guys feeling more comfortable doing things side by side than they do face to face. It's true. If you ever watch boys playing at a playground, in the sandbox, building something, eating, or even talking, you'll notice they're much more comfortable if they don't have to look directly at one another while they're doing it. A lot of behavioral therapists say that the best way to talk to a guy is in the car.

Check it out for yourself. When guys sit in the lunchroom, we are usually sitting side by side, staring out into space. Girls are comfortable sitting across from one another or even next to one another, but turned so that you are face to face. Most girls don't have a problem with eye contact, even for longer periods of time. In fact, it makes you feel more connected.

Sometimes I'll walk over to a guy in class and kneel down across from his desk, look him straight in the eye, and say, "Tell me what she said! What happened?" Guess what happens? Guys look away, their faces get red, and they squirm around and back up their chairs. They look extremely uncomfortable. Their hearts are racing, they feel nervous, and they are thinking about whatever possible way they can get out of there!

Like it or not, that's just the way guys are. We like sitting at angles or even side by side, especially when it comes to talking. Other ways feel more threatening and uncomfortable.

Think about this the next time you want a guy to open up, talk more about his feelings, and feel relaxed and unthreatened while doing it. Remember that sitting face to face, being close up and personal, and having direct eye contact is not nearly as fun and natural for guys as it is for girls. It's about as much fun as spending our entire day shopping at the mall, getting a pedicure, and then talking about our feelings over ice cream—which, by the way, is *not* fun at all.

10

Guys Feel Like Impostors

In his private heart, no man much respects himself.

—Mark Twain

Hey there," said Jack, as he sat beside a beautiful girl on a park bench in front of a duck pond.

"Hi," she answered.

"Something tells me you'd like to have dinner with me tonight," Jack said.

"No thanks. I don't think you're my type."

"Not your type?" he asked with an astonished look. "What type do you like?"

"Someone kind, sensitive, sweet . . ." she began.

"Then I'm your man! I can be those things," he said, smiling.

"Someone helpful. A good listener. Someone honest . . ." she continued.

"Outstanding! I can be all those things too!" Jack said.

"And someone who's not willing to suddenly become anything I want him to be." ■

Blending In

There is something every girl should know about guys. We are pretty good at blending in wherever we go. We go with the flow so we don't stand out in ways that would make us look like dorks. In a sense, guys can be chameleons. That's because it's safer to blend in, and it often gets the results we are looking for. But girls, don't be fooled! There is something you need to know about the *hearts* of most guys.

Guys don't feel like we are acting on the outside. Because of that, **guys often feel like impostors.** On the inside, there's a lot more going on.

When I was growing up, I changed schools about every year or so. Around fifth grade I felt the need to be really cool. That was about the same time it began to matter what brand of clothing everyone was wearing, along with who was good at sports, who was the smartest, and who was going out with the best-looking girl. In sixth grade I got stuck going to a school in a wealthy district and was put into a class of "cool" kids.

My family probably didn't have more than a few hundred bucks and an apartment to our name. My mom paid the bills and worked a lot, and we got by okay for the most part. But I sure didn't own anything like the Nike Air Solo Flights that went for around $120 a pop. On top of that, I was going through my chubby phase. It was awful. I was *not* in the inner circle of "cool." In fact, I wasn't in the outer circle either. Not even close.

To say that the other guys were hard on me would be an understatement.

So I spent a lot of time trying to act like them. I tried not to say anything stupid to let people know that I was clueless about sports teams. I spent so much time trying to fit in that I couldn't really say much about myself, except that I was spending all of my time and effort trying to be like others. And I wasn't that different. This is what a lot of guys are trying to do.

If guys were nice to one another, and *that* was considered cool, your world and our world would be an entirely different place. You would understand guys a lot better. But the fact is, that's not the way of the world. Teenage guys typically say about nine negative or sarcastic comments for every one positive or encouraging comment. They are in a day-to-day struggle to find their place in the world, just like you. They're trying not to screw up and look like idiots. Most of the time, they do it by acting like the guys around them.

Guys usually don't feel free to be who God made us. All of this makes us feel like caged birds wondering if we'll ever be free. It's a constant struggle.

Most girls I interact with in class are pretty honest about their insecurities, fears, and joys. But most guys aren't that way. It's harder for guys to accept that they don't have things figured out. It's even harder to keep all of that stuff bottled up inside.

HERE'S A SECRET:

When teenage guys are alone, they often feel like phonies. They aren't the confident beings they work so hard at trying to show to others. Guys are afraid that other guys won't like them or that you won't like them. They're terrified of finding out how girls will ▼

react to the real person inside of them. They're confused. Teenage guys are just struggling to get through the day in that circus they call high school.

It's so important for guys to feel like they're "cool" that they spend a lot of time trying to get people to affirm it. Just know this: if a guy spends lots of time trying to act cool, it's probably because he really is acting. If guys need people to pay attention to them, it's usually because they are unsure of themselves.

Most guys are all in the same boat—they just don't always know which way they are supposed to row.

Jock Schools

I love going to a certain high school to teach the guys about health education. It's one of the top schools in the state for sports, so the guys have a reputation for really being tough. They think football is the epicenter of the universe and that nothing is more important.

> One teenage boy to another: "My dad had a long talk with me about girls last night. He doesn't know anything about them either."

When you get them in a room together away from girls, turn up the truth dial, and start talking about sex and relationships, things get interesting. You can learn almost everything you need about the testosterone-driven male. Here are some interesting notes I've taken during my visits there (and at other schools like it):

Funny Things About Jock Schools:

They stink! Really, guys can smell pretty gross.

Guys are unsure of themselves.

Guys give short answers.

Guys don't talk about love.

There is no hugging whatsoever.

Guys think passing gas is the coolest thing since the invention of football.

Guys don't talk about relationships as much as girls do.

"Gay" is the most common word used to describe just about everything. More utilized than words like "the," "and," and "it."

Guys are very sensitive and cover it up by being tough or quiet.

Pass them in the hall and they don't make eye contact.

A guy's world is dictated by trying to "be cool."

Guys stick their chests out, walk upright, and try to act tough.

Most guys are basically faking it.

No guy feels like he really understands girls.

Guys are afraid to say anything in class for fear of others making fun of them.

Guys never say anything nice to one another.

A guy actually likes it when someone smashes down his barriers and talks to his heart. He always says, "Thanks, man. That was really cool."

Guys' handwriting on the board is as bad as their ability to tuck in their shirt or brush their hair.

I love these guys. They are sensitive, inquisitive, and clueless. I can see that now because I'm older and high school seems like a distant memory. But there is something to be said about this school and the reason I choose to talk about them. These guys are a perfect example of this reality: **guys have a real struggle between what we feel inside and the pressure we feel to project ourselves to the world.**

> **When people are free to do as they please, they usually imitate each other.**
>
> —Eric Hoffer

Don't Believe the Tap Dance

You've got to get it into your head that guys aren't nearly as sure of ourselves as we look. Think about this before you give us too much credit for it. I think that's where there is a big disconnect between guys and girls. Girls are simply more honest about not having everything figured out. Guys aren't necessarily lying about stuff. We just don't talk about how clueless we are about things. After all, if we did that, people would find out!

> **Believe me, every man has his secret sorrows which the world knows not.**
>
> —Henry Wadsworth Longfellow

HERE'S A SECRET:

I guess it's time to spill the beans. For those of you who think guys know more than you do about life, it's just not so. Even though we try to act cool, confident, or smooth, we really don't think we are.

About half of the high school guys I speak to think they have a uterus. I'm not joking. I say, "You *don't* have a uterus?" in a tone that says, "You must be a loser if you don't!" They always answer, "I mean, yeah. Of course I do. I thought you were asking something else." Then I tell them what it means, and we all have a good laugh while I give them a hard time about thinking that they know all the answers.

Opening Up

Just like you, guys need encouragement, hope, and affirmation. While we want the world to think that we can lift hundreds of pounds, hit home runs, and fix anything that's broken, we can't. We want to know about you just as much, or more, than you do about us.

To give you an example, here's a letter I received from one of the guys in a high school class I was teaching:

Hey Chad,

Today you came and taught my class about sex and relationships. It got me thinking about some stuff.

I used to have a big dating rotation. I didn't understand girls, but I felt better if they told me they liked me. The more girls who would go out with me, the better.

Anyway, you said the main reason girls have sex is all about love, but that after sex they just felt guilt. It made me wonder if all these girls doing stuff with me are doing it because they love me and think it will make me love them back? Because I don't. And I sure never thought about them feeling guilty before. It really hit me hard.

Recently, I was out with my friends, and I met a girl who was so nice and lots of fun. I loved to be around her. Then my feelings for her grew deeper. I think she might be really special. But she told me that I act too much like a big, tough guy who just uses girls.

I just want to be around her, but I dunno. I guess I'm just nervous to actually have to put myself out there for someone who thinks I'm like that. The fact is that I don't always want to be that way—it's just easier most of the time.

Anyway, how do I go about asking her out next time I see her? It sure would be nice to go out with someone I felt that way about. But I'm afraid of "putting my neck out there." What do you think I should do?

Later. Peace,

Mike

Nobody likes getting hurt, and guys are scared to death of it! When we fall, we fall hard. So we puff out our chests and act macho and pretend we don't have a care in the world. But below all this, we wish that someone would see us for who we really are.

There is a difference
between imitating
a good man and
counterfeiting him.

—Benjamin Franklin

Guys and Commitment

Kevin and Sarah, a young couple, were sitting on a porch swing. Sarah asked, "Kevin, do you think my eyes are beautiful?"

Kevin answered, "Yep."

After a few moments: "Kevin, do you think my hair looks good?"

Again Kevin answered, "Yep."

After a while: "Would you say that I have a gorgeous figure?"

Once again Kevin answered, "Yep."

"Oh, Kevin," Sarah said. "You say the nicest things." ■

Figster and Figette

Do you remember the first guy, Adam? He was Eve's buddy. They run around in fig leaves in all the pictures— Figster and Figette. You can learn a lot from their story.

I thought I knew the story of Adam and Eve backward and forward. God makes the earth, and *poof!* In six days, it's done. God creates all the mountains and animals and then makes a dude from the dirt. This guy is naked and happy, but then it turns out he's lonely.

So God sends Adam to surgery, takes out a rib, and *bam!* He gets Eve as his companion. They really dig each other and frolick around the Garden of Eden like two naked hippies. Eventually, they eat the bad apple, and suddenly we're all subject to war, murder, jealousy, stealing, insecurity, greed, and cheating. The stuff they call sin. Great. Thanks a lot!

One day, I was reading a book by Donald Miller, a favorite author of mine, who wrote something about this story that changed everything about my understanding of guy-girl rela- tionships.[1] It's been there from the start, so simple that it was easy to overlook.

What did God do after Adam discovered he was lonely? Most people would answer that God created Eve. No! God did something much, much wiser. Why? **Because God knew that you don't just give a guy what he wants when he wants it.** Nothing very good comes from that.

Instead, God told Adam to work. God said, "Why don't you go and name every animal on the planet?" Wow! That must have been hard to take. Adam needed a companion, and God told him to be a zookeeper. Did you ever think about how many animals there are on this planet? Good luck find- ing the leopards, and check out that perfume on those skunks.

By the way, don't let the lions eat you. Have a good time, Adam, and bring back some moose droppings!

I'm sure Adam was psyched. I'll bet he was wondering why he hadn't thought of it first! He was probably too busy chasing down monkeys. I wonder how long it took him to name all the animals. And it's not like he had the little woman to come home to after a long day of avoiding snake and alligator bites. Nope. Remember, he was lonely!

When Adam finally finished this monumental task, he fell asleep and woke up next to a gorgeous naked woman made from his own rib! He had to have been dumbstruck. He must have stared at her for days. After looking at baboons for years, he was probably just a little more than appreciative—definitely more than if he'd gotten what he wanted right when he wanted it.

All this is to say that *you* are Eve. *You* are not to be given to any guy exactly when he wants you. Guys appreciate stuff a lot more when we have to earn it or win it. We like prizes and the feeling of earning something.

TOTALLY TREASURED

Make sure that a guy knows your rules and that you have to be won completely. Choose to believe that you are a treasure, even when you may not feel like one. Uphold your God-given nature of being Eve to Adam . . . without, of course, eating any bad apples.

A Winner or a Dud?

So here you are, reading about guys. That's okay. Guys evaluate girls, and girls evaluate guys. We size each other up. We try to decide if we want to go on dates, just be friends, come within ten feet of each other, and even marry each other.

There are great ways to do this and really crummy ways. So how do you go about it? Do you have good criteria for evaluating guys, and, more important, do your criteria work?

There's a cheesy saying that goes, "We don't plan to fail. We fail to plan." Although it's trite and overused, it's really true.

When it comes to planning your criteria for evaluating guys, you need to ask yourself if your list is going to turn out well for you, your heart, and your life. Or will it get you hurt, used, beat up emotionally, and resentful? That's why it's important to plan wisely.

There are some fairly basic things you should think about when you do this, things that will tell you whether the guy is a winner or a dud. Run through this list of questions:

1. Does he care about God being first in his life?
2. Does he care about being faithful?
3. What's his moral concern about purity?
4. Is he building a good reputation?
5. Is he maintaining balance?
6. Does he have a big muscle in self-control?
7. Is he humble and considerate of others?
8. Is he a peacemaker?
9. Is he generous?
10. Does he love things that are good?

11. Is he a follower of Christ? And what in the world does that mean to both of you?
12. Are his pants on and staying that way?

Do We Size Up?

One question guys usually ask ourselves is, "Do I have what it takes?" We like to think we have life all figured out, but we don't. We sit alone at night and doubt ourselves, just like you do. We wonder if we'll be good enough . . . good enough to make the team, make the grade, get the job, earn enough money, please our parents, and get the girl. That's important for you to understand, because it may help you comprehend a little more about why we act the way we do.

Why do the guys you know act the way they do? Do you think they're confident about themselves? Do you think they're good enough for a really wonderful girl, or are they taking whatever they can get whenever they can get it? Do they act immature and avoid commitment in their lives?

Girls are dying to know why guys have a harder time committing to things than girls do. I wish there was a perfect answer, but all guys are different. Some guys look forward to commitment, and others are terrified of it.

Take me, for example. I come from a broken family. That messes with the way I look at commitment. My parents divorced when I was seven. I have some distant memories of riding my tricycle and running to hug my dad when he pulled up in the driveway after work. I also remember my parents arguing and, after that, my sister, my mom, and I moving away. We moved around a lot, and I went to many different schools. Everything was different.

That experience shaped my opinion about commitment by making me think that it's pretty hard to make a relationship last. Winding up with someone and then not loving each other terrifies me. Even though my parents' divorce had absolutely nothing to do with me, it can't help but affect my view on life and relationships.

Some people have it much better than I did, and plenty have it much worse. All of our opinions and experiences about commitment vary. That's just something you should know. Guys are scared, excited, nervous, lonely, and searching, just like you.

Test-Drive

Here's a fun thing I do with guys. It's a perfect example of how they view this whole commitment thing. First, we have to look at the word itself:

com·mit·ment: kə-'mit-mənt; Function: noun a: an agreement or pledge to do something in the future; especially: an engagement to assume an obligation at a future date; b: something pledged; c: the state or an instance of being obligated or emotionally impelled < a commitment to a cause >.[2]

Now, let's make some sense of this idea. I ask guys to imagine that they are going to take a car for a test-drive. They can pick any type of car they want. What do you think they usually say? Right. Porsche and Ferrari are always the two top picks. Let's go with a Porsche for now.

Guys and Commitment

The guy takes the Porsche out for a test-drive. No obligations. He can drive it wherever and however he wants. It's up to him. He doesn't own it yet; he's just testing it out. There aren't any commitments. How do you think he drives it?

Here's the most common answer: "I'd drive the crud out of it!" He'd drive the car about two hundred miles an hour on the autobahn, quite recklessly, I might add. Then he'd wear the tread off the tires and get about three years of use in a twenty-four-hour period. He'd drive the car recklessly, knowing that he can give it back. Having no obligation to the car makes driving it much more fun.

After that, things change. This time the guy is *buying* the Porsche. He has to put down ninety thousand dollars of his own money for it. He's worked extra hard over the last several years, saved his money, and sacrificed his time and other things he wanted, so now he can afford his dream car. He walks into the dealership and selects the interior . . .

The car is his, in his name, and he is responsible for it. How is he going to drive it? Right! Suddenly, guys don't even sound like they're talking about a car. They call it "baby." They give it names. They drive it slowly and cautiously. They keep it clean, constantly wipe it down, and put the best gas in it. It becomes something precious to them.

Why? What's changed? It's still the same car. The difference is that the guy has made a commitment to it. That changes his entire outlook on the relationship with that car. He knows that he's responsible for the car, so he treats it differently. He treats it with the care that it deserves. And it's just a stupid car!

TOTALLY TREASURED

You are like that car. You are the valuable property a guy must earn, and you are a lot more important than some dumb car can ever be.

When All Else Fails, Read the Instructions

Girls and cars are good comparisons for understanding commitment. A guy spends time with you and goes out of his way to think about you. He buys you flowers, tries to be a better listener, and goes out of his way to make you feel special. The guy has to learn how to express his feelings to you, admit his faults, apologize to you, compliment you, learn to say "I love you," and become emotionally vulnerable to you. He has to meet your parents (which can be terrifying) and save up money to buy you an expensive ring.

All of this is part of "saving up," like a guy does when he works toward and selects a car.

One day, the guy gets down on one knee with a ring and he asks you to marry him, very similar to the decision to finally purchase the car of his dreams. Then he stands at the altar and promises to protect the car, drive it nicely in rain or shine, and never leave it outside in the cold to rust. Oops. I meant to say, he takes his marriage vows. Bottom line, he commits to something valuable.

This is where the guy realizes how precious the gift is to

him. So he decides he wants to treat and drive it wonderfully. He wants to do it well, because now it's not just something he can take back to the dealership. Or, I guess I could say, he wants to treat his new wife as a treasure, and he wants to do it right because he just made a lifetime commitment.

Don't Let Guys Test-Drive You

You are not a free ride at the car dealership of "test-drive girls." You should not be given back with a low tank of gas and a beat-up engine. **You are a precious treasure to be earned with time and love.** You are the one who makes all the calls when it comes to how that will happen. Are you going to let guys take you out and test-drive you around to see if they like you or not—just to give you back with miles already on you?

How many times have you heard other girls talk about how sick they are of just giving love? Lots of girls try to love other guys and care about them, just to discover that it isn't being given back in return. Those kinds of relationships leave you with something horrible in return—baggage. Baggage is what you take onto an airplane for your clothes, not the pain you should have to carry around forever in your heart.

GUY TIP:

I'm going to say it one more time—so much of this is up to you! Remember, sometimes curiosity kills the cat. Directions are usually followed one step at a time. Curiosity makes us want to jump from step one to step ten, only to discover we have to go back to step four because things aren't working right.

12

What Guys Really Want

God evidently does not intend us all to
be rich, or powerful, or great. He does intend
for us all to be friends.

—Ralph Waldo Emerson

Out of all the friends I had in high school, I don't
know the name of the best one I had. She was more
of a friend to me than most, because she was honest
with me.

I was in my last year of Spanish class. After three
years I could say, "Me llamo Chad," like a champ. It was
my senior year, and I was starting to feel like I was a
big deal. In Spanish we got kind of rowdy, and, more
often than not, my mouth would start to have a mind
of its own. I was in the midst of an undefeated football season, which meant I walked around about a foot
taller than I really was.

One day at the end of class, we were sitting
around on the desks waiting for the bell to ring. I was
trying to be witty and show my brilliance by chiming ▼

in on making fun of someone. I don't remember what it was, and it wasn't something horrible, but it wasn't very nice either.

Then, out of nowhere, the quiet, studious, level-headed band girl in front of me turned around. She wasn't very popular or standout-ish, but she said something that shook my world. Having overheard me tease another kid in class for no particular reason, she said very factually, and with little emotion, "I think that you're a bad person, and when other people meet you, I think they will think you're a bad person too."

In just a moment, she shortened my height by two feet. I wish I had a picture of my face right then. I wanted to cry. Her height was five foot nothing, and she was a giant. She saw right through me. She was telling me I was repulsive and unacceptable. She told me that I was not as cool as I was trying to be. I didn't even try to respond. I just slunk down into my chair, unable to speak.

The rest of the day I thought about nothing else. She'd called me out and told me the truth. For a change, I was listening. Even though I tried every way to downplay it, I knew she was right. From then on, I didn't want to be a bad person. I wanted to be more like her, even if I couldn't play a tuba. She became one of my all-time best friends. I wish I could remember her name. ■

"Man, She's Just Really Cool"

Nick is a good friend who is a really lucky guy. He's likeable, friendly, smart, and also a decent-looking fellow. Nick recently got married to a girl named Anna.

I have always liked Anna. She is a lot of fun when she hangs out with us. It is fun to see how well she and Nick get along. They have a lot of the same passions and interests.

I went over to their place one day when I was in town. We went inside and Anna was in the living room reading. Nick said something about cooking, and she laughed in a sweet sort of way—the kind of laughter a guy wants to hear from a girl when she is laughing at his jokes. Then Nick and I went upstairs to play some music in his little studio. When we got up there, I was curious to know how he felt about being married and having to share his stuff with a chick all the time.

Nick gave the most startling answer. With the most honest and dude-like sincerity, he said, "Man, she's just really cool. Really cool. It's awesome!"

My brain circuitry almost blew. When he said the word "cool," he didn't mean the word you think he meant. It was a secret version of the word that guys say just to guys and reserve for the highlight moments of life's *cool*. It was the way a guy feels when he sees a big explosion, jumps out of a plane, gets a really big scar, summits a huge mountain, or gets the keys to his first car. The use of the word in that way is really rare. Yet here Nick was, saying it about a chick—a girl he recently decided to be with for life.

Nick was acknowledging that he has an awesome friend in addition to having a wife, and that's more important than anything else in a relationship! Below the surface of all the guy stuff that goes on, guys really want and need a close friend. We crave it the same way we crave oxygen. We want . . . and need . . . a friend.

Hooking a Girl Fish

What do you think guys consider to be the two most desirable traits in a girl? Go ahead, guess! Do you think it's your looks? Confidence? Attitude? Maybe you think it's your hair color, chest size, height, or fashion sense? Make a list of all the stuff you think we find desirable, and then put them in order of what you think is the most important.

Obviously, a girl's appearance has something to do with attracting guys. But your version of the word *attractive* may be too—dare I say—shallow?

Physical attraction is just the surface stuff and has very little to do with the lasting, relationship-building qualities guys are looking for. Here's the reality. If you spend all your time and effort on physical attraction, you may hook some fish, but they won't stay on the line. That's not what keeps them interested. They'll get bored and start looking at other bait. (Notice the reference to fishing. Guys like to fish.)

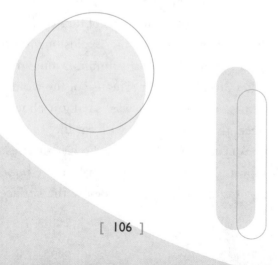

NEWS FLASH!

The two key ingredients that guys are looking for, more than anything else, are intelligence and kindness. Which ranks higher? Kindness. Guys like girls who are kind. The words *sexy, sassy, athletic, tall, short, fashionable, funny, sexual,* or *hot* are not what guys really want. If you're putting these words first in your life . . . you'll miss something. You'll miss being what we want—a kind, thoughtful, and compassionate person. When you go fishing for guys, kindness is the best bait you can put on your hook. And worms—guys like worms too.

Eye contact is incredibly important. Say you're having dinner with someone you like. Your body is doing all kinds of things your mind doesn't know about but is processing anyway. When the guy thinks the girl is intelligent, funny, and kind, his pupils dilate during the conversation. (That means the black parts of his eyeballs become almost twice their normal size!) This sets off chemical reactions in him that help his body create these weird chemicals like oxytocin and vasopressin. It's the kind of stuff that bonds people together, and they become more attracted to one another. This doesn't happen the same way when we are just physically attracted to the person. It really is the other stuff that attracts guys to you.

If you work toward anything other than your *real* personality, then you're wasting your time. If you want to become attractive to us, you can't fake it. You might be able to do it for a while, but it will catch up with you. You have to work on the things that really matter. You have to spend more time on your mind, your spirit, your heart, and how you treat other people. These are the things that make guys want you.

Here's the best part. If you're spending time on your heart, spirit, and mind, it doesn't matter if this doesn't hook someone into a long-lasting relationship. You still have good friends. And remember, you aren't looking to hook an entire school of fish. You're just looking for that special someone who will appreciate you for who you really are. You want to see if his pupils get bigger when you smile, laugh, and talk.

Friend or Foe?

I had to write an article for a magazine about the traits that guys look for in girls when they're dating. I can't speak for all guys, but I gave it my best shot anyway. After some thought, I realized there was only one thing that stands the test of time. It was the idea of companionship. A guy and girl can only hold hands and kiss so much. Even if you're the really affectionate, kissy type, you're still going to wind up spending a lot of time with a guy in a platonic way. This means friendship is going to be really crucial. You must be able to talk and communicate well together. You're going to have to like someone as much as you love him.

Sure, everyone is looking for romance, love, and affection. But those alone won't cut it. Those things are far more special if they spill out of a foundation built on friendship.

You are built with a burning desire for intimacy, and the root of it is finding a fantastic friend. This is the connection guys are looking for in everything that they do. God gave us friendship as the starting point toward intimacy. Without friendship, we will never experience real intimacy.

- How does your friendship filter look?
- Is friendship at the root of your relationships?
- Do your relationships feel more romantic than friendly?
- Are you feeling more pressure or encouragement in your relationships?
- Are you and your boyfriend compatible as great friends?
- Does the guy you're dating look beyond your appearance and see the real you?

GUY TIP:

The truth is, what a guy wants most in a girl is a friend. I realize the media blasts messages that say this isn't true. But the basis for any good relationship is the ability to be a good friend. You just need to realize what it takes to be one.

Real friends have the ability to challenge, change, and inspire you. Are you willing to let those things happen? Friends care enough to be honest with ▼

you, even when they know your faults. Friends will call to see how you're doing—not just check up on what you're doing. Friends know when you're hurting and will be there to listen—without expecting anything in return. Real friends don't look to get stuff out of the relationship for themselves. They're willing to put your needs above their own.

Brothers and Sisters in Christ

I recently read a book that I didn't like much. I don't like it when people provide their opinions as the unarguable truth with no other answer. It sounds rigid and mean, and when I think of God, that's not how I hear his voice. There was, however, one thing in the book that was fantastic.

The book spoke of relationships and pointed out an idea that stuck in my mind for days. It talked about how much better off teens might be if they stopped treating each other like potential dates. What if guys and girls tried to see and treat each other like brothers and sisters in Christ? I thought about it for a while, then—wow! What if you really did stop thinking in terms of romance and love and just started viewing others as if they were your brothers or sisters?

> True friends don't spend time gazing into each other's eyes. They may show great tenderness towards each other, but they face in the same direction—toward common interests and goals—above all, a common Lord.
>
> —C. S. Lewis

I think if we would try this, we would see one another in a different light. Instead of seeing other people for what they can offer us, we would view one another for the valuable beings that God made us to be. Not only would we appreciate others to a greater extent, but the people being valued would feel more important too.

Give it some thought. If you didn't look at the opposite sex through the lens of romance and love first but started looking at guys through the lens of friendship and care, perhaps all of your relationships would be stronger once they developed. I can't predict your future, but I think you'd wind up smiling a lot more!

13

Guys Have Secrets

I can't get no satisfaction.

—Mick Jagger

D o you think guys have secrets? Of course we do! We have secrets, quirks, and goofy traits. I don't think I'll get into all of the secret habits of guys, but let's explore a few of them.

Our Secret and Not-So-Secret Struggles

First of all, guys and girls struggle with different things. Sure, there are some of the same issues that we both go through. And there are some struggles that are more common for girls, like self-image, insecurity, jealousy, and gossip. Of course, all issues cross the gender lines from time to time.

I call the biggest struggles for guys the Three Horsemen: lust, greed, and anger. They are always there, knocking at our door. They're the top three plays of the week.

LUST

Youch. This is a tough one for most guys because of all the junk that we are being fed. Between the TV commercials, magazine and catalog advertisements, the Internet, and girls' clothes—it drives a guy's physical senses wild! Girls' bodies are the visual stimuli of the guy's universe.

GREED

Money is power. Guys sense that at a very early age. It starts in the form of simple competition. As we grow, we see how that translates into the stuff we're good at, and it can become a very bad habit. For a guy, the power to compete lasts a lifetime. It's not a bad thing, but most bad things are good things in the wrong amounts or at the wrong times. After high school and college, guys continue to compete with one another by trying to obtain more power, control, and money. Since money is a powerful way to control things, it can become like a drug.

ANGER

Guys are full of testosterone that has no place to go. It's a bit like a bull sitting in a rodeo chute. It causes anger, rage, fighting, aggression, and all the stuff you see us dealing with on the outside that makes us act in odd ways. God gave guys a warrior spirit, and when we don't learn to control our natural desire for strength, it turns into anger.

Simple or Complex?

Do you think guys are fairly simple beings or more complex? Here's what one counselor had to say: "Guys often joke about females being hard to understand, but it's rare for girls to laugh about the mysterious ways of guys. Maybe that's because girls don't realize that guys *are* complex. When a girl only takes a guy at face value, she may unknowingly sabotage a potential friendship with him before it has time to develop. Or, she may end up feeling hurt unnecessarily."[1]

That's what happens in the following story.

I had a huge crush on Andy. He was all I thought about. He seemed interested in me too. When he said he'd call, I stayed home that night and expected him to call. I wasn't going to miss it for anything! But the hours dragged by, and the phone didn't ring. Finally, when I couldn't stand waiting any longer, I called him. He was nice but seemed eager to get off the phone. I could hear his friends laughing in the background. Andy was having fun without me. I was annoyed and hurt.

Even though that young lady was pining away for her friend, Andy didn't seem to be suffering too much while waiting to see her again.

How do you know if a guy is interested or not? Here are a few insights about guys that can help answer that question. Just a few more secrets to let you know a bit more about us . . .

Guys' Lives Don't Revolve Around Girls

I hate to break any hearts here, but I've gotta give it to you straight. Guys don't think about girls 24-7. Don't get me wrong. Guys think about girls—a lot! But even if we are interested in a girl, we'll still want to have a blast with our buddies. Teenage guys don't depend on relationships the same way girls do. They tend to have more of a balance in the things they do, like sports and hobbies, their accomplishments and jobs, and in spending time with their other guy friends. During teen years, guys place a high value on the camaraderie of other guys. Which brings up another secret . . .

Guys Like Breathing Room

Guys don't appreciate it when girls isolate us from our friends. There's almost nothing that gets to guys more than a girl who takes him away from his friends all the time. On top of that, when a guy breaks up with a girl who has been possessive, it can be difficult for him to be accepted back in his circle of friends because he initially "ditched" them for her. Plus other guys will keep their distance from her. A girl with a special interest in a guy would be wise not to insist on occupying all of his time.

There's an added benefit to "sharing" a guy with his buddies. Being nonpossessive is another one of those mysterious traits about a girl that guys really like! When a girl is relaxed and enjoying life, it makes her that much more attractive.

Guys Are Vulnerable

It's a myth that guys are hard-hearted. People may call us cold, tough, and unemotional, but that's not true.

It's true that most guys don't think in terms of romantic daydreams, but we are capable of deeply caring for a girl and getting hurt just as easily as you can. Sensitive emotions can be even more painful to deal with for guys than girls, because society doesn't give us the freedom to vent our feelings. As a result, we don't express ourselves easily and keep a lot inside. But our emotions are still there!

The way a guy responds to his feelings is different from the way a girl handles them. (Remember, guys go to great lengths to avoid being teased.) Instead of crying or confiding in a buddy, a guy is more likely to do something physical, like shooting hoops or hitting a punching bag.

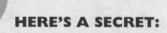

HERE'S A SECRET:

Most teen guys know they aren't ready for marriage. So they hang out with their buddies as a coping mechanism. They realize that the more they hang out with a girl, the more serious the relationship is likely to get. The more serious it gets, the more likely it's going to lead to the idea of marriage or a broken heart. So hanging out with his buddies is sort of like a guy's way of subconsciously protecting himself. And by doing that, a guy winds up protecting you as well as himself.

Here's some advice straight from teen guys. It may make you laugh, but it may also help you learn a little more about them.

- Don't always ask guys what they're thinking unless you're prepared to discuss topics such as navel lint, fire, football formations, and monster trucks.

- If you ask a question you don't really want an answer to, expect the answer you don't want to hear.

- Sometimes guys are not thinking about you. Live with it.

- If guys are going somewhere, absolutely anything they wear is fine. Really.

- Crying feels like blackmail to guys.

- Ask for what you want. Let's be clear on this one: Subtle hints don't work. Strong hints don't work. Really obvious hints don't work. Just say it!

- Guys are not mind readers, and they never will be. Their lack of mind-reading ability is no indication that they don't care or think about you.

- "Yes" and "no" are perfectly acceptable answers to almost every question.

- Come to guys with a problem only if you want help solving it. That's what guys want to do. Sympathy is uncomfortable for them, especially as teens.

- It's neither in your best interest nor theirs to take any quiz together.

- You can either ask guys to do something or tell them how you want it done. Not both.

- If guys ask what's wrong and you say "nothing," they will act like nothing's wrong. They know you're lying, but it's just not worth the hassle. Say what you mean.

- If guys say something that can be interpreted in two ways and one of those ways makes you angry, they meant the other way.

14

Dating Advice from Guys

The purpose of opening a door for a girl is not because she can't do it for herself. Remember this. It's not about a guy asserting his power and authority. It's about a guy showing honor and respect for you. When he asks you out, pays for stuff, and opens doors for you, it's just his way of showing you that you're valued. It's not about him. It's about his being selfless and thinking about you. That should tell you something about his character. ■

Who Asks Who Out?

Do you believe in equal rights? Well, I hope not *entirely*. Now, hear me out. I don't think we really want to have guys and girls doing all of the exact same things. When two people dance, one of them has to lead; otherwise, they'll both wind up with bruised feet looking sort of dumb. Neither will enjoy the dance.

Sometimes guys and girls have different roles. As it turns out, most girls prefer that guys ask them out. So don't lower your standards just because you feel the pressures of "contemporary" relationships. That doesn't mean anything. Don't think that guys have given up on romance. Following the crowd is usually just a matter of the blind following the blind.

Don't get me wrong. I'm not trying to make a concrete rule that girls should never ask guys out. But I think it's safe to say that it just tends to work out a little better, flow a little easier, and may be a bit more romantic if a guy does the asking. Here's why: guys need to work up the courage to do it. They aren't just born with it.

HERE'S A SECRET:

As much as guys want to act confidently, it takes a lot of nerve to ask a girl out. So let us do the work. We're building up our confidence muscle. It's not a good idea to keep guys from building the muscles that we will need all our lives anyway. It also lets you know that we are interested in you and that we're willing to stick our necks out to hear your answer of yes or no.

If there are any such things as balance and power, making the decision of saying yes or no puts the power right back into your hands anyway.

Lots of girls think it's no big deal to ask a guy out because it's the getting to know each other that's important. While there is some truth in that, there is also some truth in the way that guys view girls who ask them out. If a guy can see that a girl already is really interested in him, it may change his whole opinion of her.

Another reason to let guys ask you out is that a guy feels good about himself when he finally musters up the courage to ask you out. When you answer yes, he starts to think about how to make it a good date. He gets more excited about his date with you if he has to put some effort into the whole thing.

In general, it's a good rule of thumb to let guys do the instigating. It doesn't mean that you both can't enjoy the dance. It just means that things may go smoother if each person knows what the other is supposed to be doing. Besides, guys need to learn how to dance anyway!

Group Dates

Remember, the most important thing you can get out of dating in high school is learning the value of friendship. Most likely, you and your high school sweetheart aren't going to marry each other, so why put more of your heart into the relationship than you should? Take some of the dating pressure off and do things in groups.

Getting together in groups takes a bunch of pressure off needing to overdo just about anything. It's also a great way to get to know each other and have fun doing it. You can see how the guy interacts around you and your friends.

It's also a lot safer to date in groups. There really is safety in numbers, and there's also safety in the comfort and company of friends. You're free to relax with your friends while you get to know the guy you're going out with. That way, if the guy isn't all he's cracked up to be, you're still with other people you can have a great evening with. If it does go well, then you get the added bonus of knowing you like him and knowing how to have fun around him.

If you read the last chapter, you discovered that the Three Horsemen are the biggest problem areas for guys. They are lust, greed, and anger. Those things don't suddenly disappear when a guy is on a date with a girl. I'm not trying to scare you or anything like that. But I do want to point out that a guy needs to know how to keep those things in check when he's out on a date with you. What better way to find out than among friends? A group date is also a good way to keep God-honoring principles in line. When a guy and girl find themselves falling head over heels for each other, it can be hard to live up to the standards you have promised both God and yourselves you would live by. If you haven't made that promise to God and to yourself, do that before you start dating. So when in doubt, call up your friends and arrange to go out together.

An added bonus is getting to see how the guy treats you in the presence of others. You'll get to see how he treats your friends. It can be really difficult to fall hard for someone and then discover he doesn't like your friends. Then you wind up with him asking you to choose between them. Who needs that?

You Don't Owe Guys Anything

You don't owe anything about your body to anyone. After you've gone out on a date and had a good time, you should know that you don't owe the guy anything. You aren't obligated to kiss him, touch him, allow him to put his arm around you, or even let him hold your hand.

When you say yes to going out on a date, you should show the guy the respect of your time and attention. That's all you "owe."

Lots of girls feel pressure from guys while on a date. They'll give in to guys because they feel uncomfortable or insecure about saying no. Girls are sometimes afraid of making guys mad or worried that the guys won't like them in return. To be honest, what it really means is that a girl doesn't know her own self-worth. She's interested in pleasing others much too easily when she gives in.

Girls like diamonds and other fancy, pretty stuff, because these things are rare, expensive, and hard to get. Don't make yourself as easy to get as the five-dollar earrings at Wal-Mart.

Saying no doesn't make you a prude. It doesn't make you come across as shallow, freezerlike, or too uptight. The more you demand respect and set yourself apart from other girls, the more the right guy will want to put forth the time and effort to show you the respect and care you deserve.

GUY TIP:

If a guy sees that physical things come easily with you, he'll wind up disappointed in the long run. Think about it. If we have something to look forward to, we become like excited puppies waiting for someone to play fetch. It's more like a game of chess than a game of checkers. If a guy really likes you, he'll be willing to put in the time and effort without expecting physical rewards in return. If not, then he's probably acting like a jerk, and you don't really want to spend your time with him anyway.

Be a diamond in the rough. Don't put yourself on display at the discount store for any guy to purchase easily.

Honor and Regret

Most girls don't fully understand what's going on when it comes to sex. Your perspective on things is very different from a guy's. Don't worry, guys don't really get it either. When a girl is on a date, she might justify having sex by saying, "But I love him," even if she doesn't want to go through with it. Why?

The girl pictures marrying the guy someday. The guy pictures everything he wants to do with the girl before he goes back to tell his buddies about it.

Why does a guy act like that? For two reasons. First, the physical pleasure is no doubt a big plus for him. But second, because it makes him feel like a man. Yet there is a great irony in that, because what's so manly about deceiving a girl?

I have discovered that when you honor a woman, you also honor yourself. By doing what's right in his heart, and in the girl's best interest, a guy ensures that he won't have any long-lasting regrets to live with. You see, the regret will last far longer than a few moments of immediate pleasure.

WARNING!

Guys want to be honorable. Living with no regrets is better than trying to convince yourself that you don't regret the decisions you've made. There's a big difference.

Avoid Traps

It's just as important to avoid bad things as it is to look for good things. This is especially relevant in the world of dating. While it's fine to be hopeful, you shouldn't be naive.

Avoid bedrooms: As a teen, your bedroom is for sleeping and throwing your dirty laundry on the floor, not for getting to know your boyfriend. Guys have strong associations to things. If we're in a relaxed setting with a bed, we're going to associate you with that situation. You're better off staying out of the bedroom except for sleeping (alone), which I thought I should clarify. But I'm sure you got that.

Stay in public: Girls don't usually get slapped or pressured in public places. So make sure you get to decide where you want to go on dates—and make sure you go someplace where you and the guy will be around other people. Trust me, you're a lot safer that way.

Skip the party scene: Over 90 percent of the time that teenage sexual activity takes place, alcohol or drugs are involved.[1] Dating is about getting to know each other, not about partying and drinking. Alcohol distorts reality. If you like each other, why distort your physical reality? If you and the guy don't like each other much, why are you going out in the first place? Nothing good can come from drinking or drugs, so avoid them altogether. These substances sure aren't a trigger for romance.

The creepy dude: You may not always know someone well when you're asked out on a date. If that's the case, don't accept a random invitation from him, even if he doesn't seem creepy. If you don't really know someone and, more important, his character, then don't say yes to a date and certainly don't fly solo. If you do accept an invitation to go out, then agree only if he's willing to double-date or go out with a group of your friends. You can still have a great time. After getting to know him better, then you can decide if he's nice enough to see again or if the dude just needs to move on without you.

That's Somebody Else's Wife

Most of the girls I've dated are now married to other men. When I put myself into the shoes of those men, I wish I hadn't done what I did with their wives. In fact, I feel like I need a good punch in the nose.

So it goes without saying that when I get married, I'm not going to like the idea that someone else has made all kinds of romantic or sexual memories with my wife.

What about you? Do you like the idea of someone else being with your future husband? Take it a step further. After you're married and have your own children, how will you feel about a guy taking advantage of your daughter?

I see girls from a much different perspective now. Every one of you is someone else's daughter. You're someone else's future wife. You were each made by God as his special treasure, perhaps someday to be shared in one very special relationship with just one man. Who am I to get involved and screw all that up?

Meet My Dad

Be sure to introduce the guy you are dating to your parents, especially to your dad. I hope you have a loving mother and father. If your dad isn't involved in your life the way he should be, allow your mom to serve in both roles. If you have neither, choose an adult who loves you.

I'm not asking you to set up a double-date with your folks. Just let the guy know that you are someone's very important daughter. When a guy sees the

> If, by chance, your dad has big arms, tell him to wear a tight T-shirt just to let a guy know that those arms could hurt his face if he hurts his daughter. Your date would do the same thing for his daughter when the time comes.

person who loves and protects you, buys your clothes and your food, and is involved in your life, the date will be different. Here's why. He thinks of you as someone's daughter, not just *his* date. He takes into consideration that it's not about getting what he wants from you, but instead he thinks about you in relation to your family.

Here's a little more advice. You may not want to get us too involved with your family too quickly. Sometimes that creates a bond that can make us feel locked into the relationship with you too fast. Just make sure that we know your parents are there for you and involved. Show us that your family is important to you and that you expect us to treat you with the care and respect that not only you, but also your family, demand.

Are We Sexually Compatible?

Sex is meant to complement a relationship, not to be the most important aspect of it. That's what I've discovered. It's supposed to be the icing on the cake when all the other aspects of your relationship are working well. I've come to understand that the sexual aspect of a relationship will be good if the rest of the relationship is good. That's why I know I don't have to sleep with my future wife to find out if we're sexually compatible. If we get along in every other area, then the physical stuff will be even better.

God and Sex

I discovered something that outdoes sex. Something and Someone. It's God.

God has finally given me the strength to wait for sex. I wish I could say that I had waited for marriage in the first place. I do have regrets, and they have lasted and will last so much longer than any momentary pleasures. I have regrets about the way I treated girls. But God has forgiven me and changed me, and he is in the process of changing me more and more every day.

God has given me the ability to wait for marriage before I have sex again. It's been a struggle at times, but God has been big enough to get me through it. All things are possible with him. As each day, week, and year goes by, I know I'll have a better and stronger marriage because I've waited. I have a stronger relationship with God as a result of depending on him in this vital area of my life as a man.

I realize that some of you reading these words have already made mistakes in your relationships. If you are currently sexually active with your boyfriend, or if you have been sexually active in the past, *stop*—today! God always offers us forgiveness and the encouragement to make better decisions. No matter what you've done in the past, with God's help you can restore a pure heart and mind in your relationships until you are married.

God is the author of sex, love, and relationships. He created these things for us to enjoy when we fully follow his design for how things should be done. I've come to discover that God is not a "moralizer." He doesn't say, "Do this" or "Don't do that" for no reason. When God says, "Wait for marriage to have sex," he's not trying to show us who's the boss. He's saying it because he loves us and it's in our best interest. He's saying it because he knows how he built us, knows what's best for us, and knows what will bring us the *most* fulfillment.

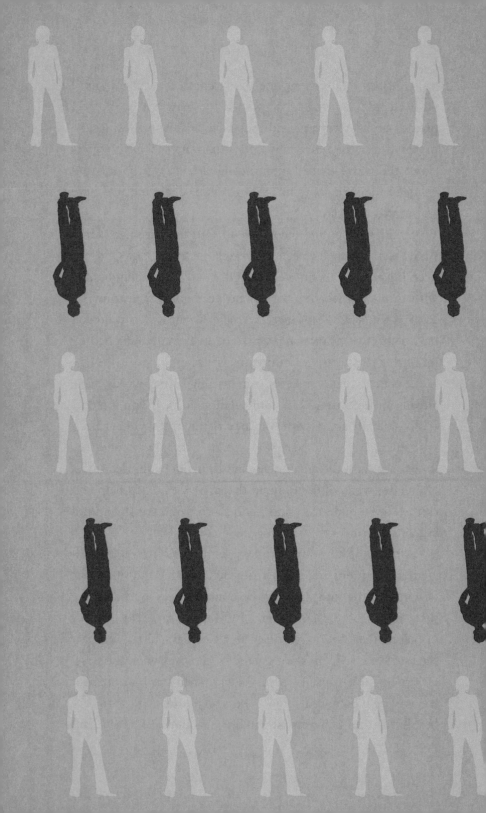

Barbie and GI Joe

Wisdom is the most important thing; so get wisdom. If it costs everything you have, get understanding.

—Proverbs 4:7

15

Why They Aren't Friends

If two people agree on everything,
one of them is unnecessary.

—Anonymous

GI Joe and Barbie dashed off to save a soldier being held captive in a jungle hut. They escaped giant explosions and dodged flying bullets as they rescued their friend. Once they untied him, they sneaked out of the hut and jumped into a boat waiting for them to make their escape. They tore down the river and plunged over a waterfall. They were thrust onto dry land by the rush of the white water, just in time to jump into the small cargo plane waiting to take them to safety. As they stumbled into the plane with only a few flesh wounds, Barbie and Joe grabbed each other's hands and squeezed. They'd made it!

The plane delivered them to Barbie's pink convertible. She dropped off their friend and drove to their pretty pink house where they washed up for dinner. After a luxurious bath, Barbie met Joe back in front of the fire where they hugged and kissed for hours. Barbie showed Joe some new khaki pants she'd ▼

bought on sale for him earlier in the day. He tried them on and they fit wonderfully. They had a candlelit dinner and talked for hours and hours. What a day! ■

Opposites Attract?

Have you seen that episode of GI Joe and Barbie? If you have, please shoot me an e-mail and let me know where I can find it!—Yeah, I didn't think so. If Barbie and GI Joe ever hung out, one of them would end up dead. I don't mean just *slightly* dead. I mean dead as a doornail. Why? Because they are complete opposites.

Think about it. Barbie, who is what . . . nine feet tall in her pink sequin airline attendant outfit, wouldn't exactly fit in with jungle machetes, grenades, mud, and really bad body odor. Not to mention good old Joe, who would have a pretty hard time at Barbie's tea parties while hanging out in the Hamptons. I highly doubt he'd be willing to wear pink polo shirts with checkered shorts underneath all of his camouflage.

Can you see it? GI Joe, Barbie, and her other man, Ken, sitting around drinking iced tea at patio parties, then jogging in slow motion along the beach together? Maybe Ken could show Joe how to pop his collar and tie a sweater around his waist or shoulders. Naturally, Joe could show Ken how to go to the bathroom in the jungle where they have to bury their waste, eat bark, and crawl around in the mud. Top it all off by rigging a raccoon with some explosives and blowing up a whole shack full of bad guys!

To be honest, I don't know why someone hasn't brought

these three characters together in some wonderful situation comedy. After all, they're almost perfect . . .

Okay, enough! I don't have to tell you why Barbie and GI Joe *aren't* friends. They're just too entirely different. They don't exist in the same world. And while they don't resemble everything that goes on between guys and girls, they do serve to illustrate one very important point. **Guys and girls are very different.**

This is a fact that we often underestimate. Sure, there are similarities. We all like to eat, we all sleep, we all want to be loved, and we may even have a fondness for kittens or puppies. Most of us laugh a little when someone falls down. Or is that just me? Hmm . . .

Guys and girls are just different—very different. How are we different? And what's the point of knowing those differences? For starters, it's fun! You don't have cooties anymore, right? I hope not. And if you don't, then you're probably fascinated by how guys and girls are different from one another. Don't worry. You're not alone.

IT'S A MYSTERY!

The truth is, your sexuality as a guy or girl affects your behavior. The way you display these differences makes you distinctly male or female. I'm not telling you what to do with these differences. I'm just saying there are some. There is a purpose for even the smallest differences between guys and girls. But we'll get to that later.

You Jane . . . Me Tarzan

Here are some simple yet funny things that I've noticed about the differences between most girls and guys:

1. Girls generally use restrooms as social experiences. Guys won't speak a word or even make eye contact with other guys they don't know while using them. However, girls can meet, cry, share life experiences, and laugh together like old friends by the time they leave.

2. A girl's hair can be fourteen inches long, yet she expects her friends to notice when it is cut by just a quarter inch.

3. When a girl looks in the mirror, she will often focus on one tiny imperfection. Girls may obsess about one area of their body they think is too fat. A dude, on the other hand, can be three hundred pounds, white as a ghost, with odd body hair, and smell like something awful, but will focus on the one developed area of his biceps.

4. A guy will pay two bucks for an item only worth one if he really needs it. A girl will pay one dollar for a two-dollar item that she doesn't need, because it looks so cute and it's on sale.

5. A guy may have up to five items in his bathroom. The average number of items in a girl's bathroom is reported to be as high as 437.

6. A guy's handwriting is often ugly and unreadable. Do you know what else? We're okay with it. In fact, I can

safely say that most of us even like it. Girls, on the other hand, will pull out their scented, colored markers and matching stationery and use these enormous loops to finish off every letter. And just so you know, it's hard to understand what a girl is saying, because even if she's dumping us, she'll finish off her note with a big smiley face and colored hearts at the end.

7. Girls are fascinated by shoes. In general, this is very, very, very confusing to males.

8. Guys expel gas . . . but girls don't like it. What they don't know, however, is that for every bit of gas that slips out, the guy has successfully held it in for fifteen minutes, enduring excruciating pain in the process.

These are just a few differences to kick around and start thinking about when it comes to guys and girls. Let's proceed with a few more, a bit more in-depth.

Room to Groom

Without looking at anybody else, take a look at your fingernails. Go ahead. Look at them. Okay, how did you do it? Did you extend your hand out flat with your palm facing down to look at your nails? Did you look at both hands? The fact is, about eight in ten times, girls will look at their hands this way.

> People throw away what they could have by insisting on perfection, which they cannot have, and looking for it where they will never find it.
>
> —Edith Schaeffer

All I really asked you to do is look at your nails, but what did you do? You probably looked at the entire presentation—your hands, your fingers in proportion to your hands, your fingers in comparison to your nails, the jewelry adorning your wrists and fingers, the cuticles surrounding your nails, whether or not you have a hangnail, and possibly the color of your nails and how the polish looks. You may have even looked at all of this in proportion to your arms, along with the tone and shade of your skin on your arms—how long your arms are, if you need to go tanning or may need more sun, and how your shirt balanced everything else out—because, after all, it is the closest thing you're wearing that may have an effect on your nails, particularly if they are polished! Oh . . . and you may have noticed that your nail polish is chipped and in need of replacing. And what about fake nails? Nah. Forget that, I don't even want to go there.

By now, you've more than gotten my point anyway. Ask a guy to look at his fingernails. What will he do? About eight in ten of us will curl our fingers into our palms, then turn our palms upward, and bring our nails close to our face. We will look at our fingernails only because you asked us to do it. What we will *not* do is have a clue as to why we are supposed to be looking at them. Guys don't color-coordinate, and most of us don't even know what cuticles are. We look at our nails and say, "Yep, they're nails. I have them. I guess I'm glad I got 'em!" Well, most likely not the last part. That was a real stretch.

Now don't worry if you happened to do it that way too. You're not a strange, nail-looking-at-backward, crazy-handed freak of a girl. Honest. In general, girls tend to be into grooming a whole lot more than guys. It probably doesn't take you a ton of research to understand that. Just smell a guy after he hasn't showered for a day, and you'll see that he doesn't usually keep up with the girls in that category! Wait a minute— I think I want to save you from smelling a guy who hasn't showered for a day. Maybe you should just take my word for it? Much safer.

If you have a brother, the odds are that your room smells way better than his room does. You probably have more nail polish and hairbrushes, that's for certain. We do notice all those little details, even when it comes to fingernails. You need room to groom, and chances are you need a lot more room to groom than guys do. We just don't care about our physical appearance the same way.

The Treat and Greet

There's the crazy, high-pitched, screaming "Hello!" that girls do. And then there's the guys' fabulous ghetto gangsta greeting, where we have to hug with one hand 'cause we could hit you with the other. These are the differences between guys and girls, which come out even when we say hello to each other.

For example, I was in the coffee shop when two girl-friends saw each other. I'm guessing that they hadn't seen each other in quite a while. Immediately, their voices went from calm to a freakish, high-pitched, alien-intriguing, dogs'-ears-hurt squeal. At least that's what it sounded like to me. Girls would probably call it excitement and happiness. They jumped up and down and squealed some more. Apparently, they weren't fighting, but I couldn't figure out what the big deal was. They were just saying hi.

Girls and guys greet each other in incredibly different ways. Guys usually say hi with little to no emotion whatsoever. We do this especially as teenagers. We don't have the same confidence in expressing our emotions that girls do. So we act "cool" instead. Allow me to demonstrate:

"What's up, playa?"

"Hey."

"What's up, man?"

"Yo."

Head nod.

Don't forget the turn-it-into-a-fist, finger-trickle-off way guys shake hands. If we ever hug, it's not really an embrace. It's this weird, awkward, try-to-be-cool-looking slapping of the hands between us, while we grab the guy's shoulder with the other hand. What's important is not so much to embrace but to pat each other two or three times on the back—and violently too. It's as if the embrace is saying, "I love you, but I might hit you, too, because I'm tough but full of love." I suppose it could be called a tough-love hug.

Girls, you have permission to laugh.

Playing with Fire . . . Yea!

Why in the world are guys so obsessed with fire . . . and then there's blowing stuff up . . . shooting off fireworks . . . or just shooting in general—paintball, BB guns, arcade games, and laser tag? Why don't most girls try to set things on fire, make contraptions that blow things up, or try to put M-80s into bluegills to see how far their guts will fly?

There's a reason. Most guys like dangerous things. We like taking risks. We like to spike our adrenaline levels. When we're excited but scared at the same time, we feel very alive. Being in thrilling and dangerous situations is a way a guy builds confidence, overcomes fears, and feels as though he's a guy among guys. Sure, it's a little strange to you, but it's an important way for a guy to find his identity as a man.

I don't mean to break any hearts here, and I doubt I will, but a guy is not someone who is just kind, sweet, and smells good all the time. He is a warrior, a stud, a tough *and* caring person. As they say in the movie *Braveheart*, which is all about guys, he is a warrior-poet. He is both a warrior and a poet.

Guys do all kinds of stuff that might seem weird or odd to you, but know that it does have a place. After all, you do all kinds of stuff that we think is pretty strange too. C'mon, it's true. But GI Joe and Barbie have to learn to get along, despite their differences. He must wash his dirty hands and eat with a fork, and she has to wear a camouflage dress to dinner. Hey, maybe that's a new doll that would sell!

What to Do?

There are lots of differences between girls and guys, and we could go on about them forever. Some are fun, some are goofy, and some have seemingly nothing to do with answers to your questions about guys. But there is a bigger point.

If guys and girls look at fingernails differently, imagine how differently we see everything else. We probably see dating differently. We probably carry our emotions differently. We most likely have different ways of loving one another and being loved by one another. Bottom line is that guys and girls will act, think, and feel differently in many ways.

Many folks look at differences negatively. Sure, some of them you can laugh about. But most everyone draws his or her own conclusion about things that are different before trying to understand them.

You may not understand why a guy won't open up to you about what he's thinking. Maybe you're confused about why he gives you little gifts when all you really want are his words. For that guy, those gifts *are* the words you're seeking. That's because guys and girls communicate in different languages. That code just needs to be unlocked and understood for each person.

The more we understand one another, the better off we'll be. More important, this stuff relates to advice we get from the Bible. Take a look at the different ways Jesus was able to communicate with and forgive sinners.

In one story, Jesus's disciples were trying to preach to some townspeople. It wasn't going well. People weren't listening. They had hardened hearts and chose to reject Jesus's teachings. They were getting angry, rude, and hostile. What did Jesus do in response? The Bible says that Jesus looked at them with compassion. Jesus saw them as "sheep without a shepherd" (Matthew 9:36).

Jesus didn't walk away from people because of differences. He tried to understand why they were different, and he knew that they needed compassion in response.

GUY TIP:

The next time a guy is acting weird, annoying, or just plain different . . . stop and look at him through the eyes of Jesus. Try to understand why he is behaving that way.

Why They Aren't Friends

You've gotten a lot of information so far. Before you head into the remaining chapters, stop to catch your breath. Take a few minutes to reflect on the answers to these questions:

1. When you look in the mirror, who do you see?

2. When you look in the mirror, what do you think needs to change, and why?

3. What do you think guys see when they look at you?

4. What do you want guys to see when they look at you?

5. What are you looking for in a relationship?

6. What are the things that scare you the most about relationships?

7. What's your idea of the perfect relationship?

16

Extra! Extra!
Hear All About It!

*Our eyes work ... usually more
than we ask them to.*

—Chad

Rachel has a problem. She can't figure out what's wrong with guys! "What's the deal with them anyway? It's like they're just trying to get something from you or hook up with you. They don't care about anything else! I'm not a slut, and I don't have a sign advertising sex around my neck. I just want a guy who likes me for who I am—someone I can care about and like in return. Why do I always attract such jerks?" ■

It's Easier Than You Think

Have you ever listened to a friend vent or found yourself venting about annoying guys? (It's okay if you have.) Have you wondered why you or a girlfriend seem to be getting the attention of, or having relationships with, guys who aren't respectable, polite, song-singing heroes or drop-dead gorgeous romantics who just want to hold your hand and tell you how beautiful you are? All right, maybe that's a little much.

Here's my point. Many times (emphasis on *many*) guys hear girls talking about their frustrations with guys. Girls are ticked off that guys obsess about the physical and don't focus on the heart of a girl. It's as though girls feel like they are magnets for creepy, immature, self-centered guys. And the worst part is . . . they are clueless as to why!

As you can probably guess on your own, there are many reasons for that. Some that you're likely aware of; some you may not be. So turn off your "girl brain" and try to look at things through a guy's eyes for a bit. It will be okay . . . it's probably easier than you think!

An Almost Creepy Memory . . .

Mike is twelve, going on thirteen, and hanging out with some buddies. One of the guys pulls out a magazine, but not just any magazine. It's *Playboy*. Mike's heart starts beating very quickly at the sight of those letters, because he knows what's inside. He flips past the articles that some guys claim to read and heads straight to the pictures. Sure enough, he sees a beautiful, naked, flawless (airbrushed), smiling, inviting, seemingly perfect woman. She is just lying there, inviting him into this fantasy world. Mike's brain is forever different.

Mike is now sixty-five. That's right, sixty-five. Over fifty years have passed since that memorable day. There is something that you don't know about his brain. Mike can still recall about thirteen different parts of that picture he saw when he was just a teenager. It's true. On average, his brain can still recall at least thirteen aspects of the picture.

It's very hard to understand how guys' brains can have such a lasting memory of an experience so small, so long ago. Maybe it doesn't concern you a great deal, or maybe it just grosses you out to know that.

Why are guys so obsessed with girls' bodies? Is that all we care about? The answer is . . . **yes**! Especially if girls let us be obsessed with their bodies, guys will continue to react that way. We honestly don't want to be that way at heart, but a guy's mind and heart are often in conflict with each other.

The good news is that our decisions aren't all up to us. Some are actually up to you, especially the ones that concern *your* body. Let me explain this in another way.

Imagine that you are a guy. A girl walks into the room wearing nothing but underwear or a bikini. She walks over and sits down across from you. She wants to talk about her likes and dislikes, favorite movies, books, music, and the kind of dog she owns. She's a really nice girl with a great personality. What are you thinking about?

NEWS FLASH!

Answer: Sex! Her body, her curves, legs, lips, skin, and more sex! Her body says to our brains, "Let's go!" It's because of the way our brains are designed. All people have two sides to the brain. One is for logical use and one is for visual. This part is important: If these two things are ever in conflict with each other in a guy's brain, visual wins out. That means that even if we want to get to know this girl and enjoy a conversation with her, we are too overwhelmed by her body for that to immediately happen. Our mind tells us that her body is there and it's available. Talking takes a backseat to the amount of crazy hormones that are now overwhelming our brain and body.

GUY TIP:

All of this isn't just a matter of willpower. Girls don't know this about guys, but we need you to be there to help us. Believe it or not, you can help or hurt both yourself and guys by the way you act, dress, talk, and present yourself. It's up to you to make it easier for a guy to get to know you. Do both the guy and yourself a favor ... make guys look at you and see God in you.

Buying What You Advertise

Girls like to wear cute outfits, right? That used to mean a sundress and nice shoes. Today, it's the tiny skirts that come just shy of a girl's underpants, in addition to belly shirts that show a girl's skin at both the top and bottom. Of course, there are also shirts that say, "You're at the top of my to do list!" and "Too hot to handle!" Or, "I have brains, too, not just these." And one more: "Your boyfriend likes me more!"

Why do girls wear this stuff? What does it mean to a guy? Here are the reasons I hear:

"It's cute!"

"It's trendy!"

"It's sassy!"

"Because I want to have sex and I'm telling you I'm available!"

When women go wrong, men go right after them.

—Mae West

Here's where the problem comes into play. **Guys are interested in buying what *we* think you are advertising . . . not what *you* think you're advertising.** There's a huge difference. Girls may never understand how powerful visual appearance can be to guys. That's okay, because you're not a guy. However, you need to know that *guys are guys*, so if you show us your body, we'll want your body. It's really that simple. It's extremely hard for us to have to talk, hold your hand, listen, and be a gentleman if the message we think you're sending is, "I'm available!"

Most of you aren't telling guys that with your words, but you are with your body, yet it's not what you mean. This is where our communication lines cross from what we're saying to what we're doing.

WARNING! ———————————————

If your body isn't available, don't tell guys it is by putting it on display. I'm not just talking about swimsuits at the pool. I'm talking about the scantily clothed, sexy-as-you-can-get, advertising-your-legs-and-stomach look that most girls think of as just "cute."

Guys are overwhelmed by the mixed messages we get from TV, magazines, and everything else. Our brains don't know how to handle the thousands of confusing messages. We don't need to get a message from you on top of all that saying, "My body is right here, looking available! My sexuality vibe is strong! Aren't I flirty and confident? Guess what this outfit is designed to show off? Find me sexy! Oh . . . but more than anything else, please respect me and my heart!"

When guys get the message **"I'm telling you with my body that I'm available, but I'm telling you with my words that I'm not!"** it is very confusing. Plus, guys will always lean toward the message that's showing off your body. We won't know how to care about you in the way you want to be cared about if that's the biggest message we're getting. ▼

It's not old-fashioned to respect your body. And when did being modest become a bad thing? Modesty is all about confidence and understanding that a little bit of mystery goes a long way. It means that you understand the messages you're sending and why. It shouldn't mean that you're "afraid to express yourself." It's feeling confident about who you are and not needing others to affirm your importance.

Guy Repellent

There's a big problem in our society. People think that if lots of guys like a girl, she must be hot! Alternatively, if guys don't like her, that means she's not. This kind of thinking is insane!

That's what happens when we depend on others to feel valuable. Why would you trust someone else's opinion over your own?

It's as though you're giving up on your own opinions of yourselves to be judged by others. Don't get me wrong—it's perfectly natural for all of us to want to be liked by others. When someone finds you to be attractive, wants to look at you, talks to you, and pays attention to you, it's nice! It's flattering. It's fun! It may just put some confidence in your step. But in the end, it's a sad story. Why?

Too many girls want guys to like them—note that was a plural *guys*. Not a couple of guys and not *the right guy*. If this describes you, then you need to change your thinking.

> Women who set a low value on themselves make life hard for all women.
>
> —Nellie McClung

Think about this instead. If it seems like a lot of guys don't like you, that can be a good thing! What? Yep, it's true. So how can you be likeable, attractive, smart, and not have a boyfriend? Maybe it means something else. **Instead of attracting everyone, you're simply repelling the guys who are bad for you!**

Why are girls in need of attention from so many guys? More important, does this kind of thinking have a good or bad effect on your relationships, your self-image, and your life? (The answer is *bad*.) It has a negative effect on you. You need a guy repellent.

I know this is a smack in the face of all the reality-TV freaks who believe you have to be hot, hot, hot and always have lots of dating options. But think about it. These people need a big wake-up call! It's not a healthy way of thinking. You don't need tons of guys to be attracted to you.

How many guys do you want to marry? How many do you want to date? Ten? Fifty? One hundred and fifty? You don't need tons of guys to like you. If you do, it's a telltale sign that more than likely you don't like yourself. You are not comfortable in your own skin.

If you have a healthy self-image, good self-esteem, and find your self-worth in God, you won't look to guys to give you value.

NEWS FLASH!

If you want to find answers, look toward the guy who is your perfect Father. He hangs out in heaven, and he's always ready and willing to listen. No guy on earth can really make you feel valuable. He can affirm your worth, but he can't create it. Honestly, he doesn't want to, but God does.

You have a natural guy repellent. It comes out by telling guys who you are, and by doing this, you'll naturally attract the people who will be good for you. You'll also repel the people who don't need to be a part of your life.

At the end of the day, you don't need twenty guys feeding you grapes, rubbing your feet, and playing you love songs. You just want one—the *right* one. One great guy is better than twenty guys who aren't right for you. In fact, anytime twenty guys get together to try to do anything, they end up looking like a big car-wrecked pile of dumb. Believe me. You don't want to be in that car.

The Reality of Sex

Hey, my name is Mike. You came to my class today to teach us about sex and all that stuff. I really learned a lot. I never realized that so many people get sexually transmitted diseases and all that horrible junk. I don't ever want to get that stuff. I didn't know that there were so many and how easy you could get them. It really makes you think about the girls out there. You just never know if you're really safe. It made me rethink the whole sex thing, and I came to a different decision.

I realize now that if I want to be safe, I just have to nail virgins.

This Crazy Thing Called Sex

Did you just go, "Ugh!"? I hope so. There might even be an ounce of humor in that little story if it wasn't true. I regret to inform you, it is. And that was after he sat through three days of education about sex. When I read that letter, I sat back in my chair and just said, "Wow." Just when I think I've heard it all, I am always surprised at how clueless guys can be about sex. So welcome to the reality of sex.

If you're like most teens, this is either the first or one of the first pages you turned to in this book. What does that mean? You're human. You are a lovely, beautiful human who is interested in this crazy thing called sex.

First of all, this chapter isn't a how-to manual on sex. Instead, let's just explore what both guys and girls think about, say about, and do about sex. It's vital that we try to understand this subject that's no longer considered "hush-hush." You can't avoid it and you definitely can't ignore it, because it's everywhere.

One of the devil's greatest tricks is to take God's amazing gifts and distort them so he can use them against us. Isn't it funny how sin can be something good and natural that is simply done at the wrong time or in the wrong context? Sex is exactly like that. It is a great gift. It's also the pollution of our culture, because we have changed our understanding of it. Let's take a closer look.

First of all, I want to apologize to you. I am sorry about today's culture and the way that you and your friends are being taught about something as great as sex. I'm sorry that there are so many people trying to use sex to sell you garbage. I'm sorry that the movies and media tell you that sex is just another thing you have to deal with these days.

I'm sorry that you aren't being told how incredibly important and precious you are, and how much you have to offer to others just for being you. I'm sorry that adults tell you that you're not in control of your own hormones and that your sex drive is no more controllable than your family dog. I'm sorry that people say, "Boys will be boys" and that they say sex is just another part of life.

TOTALLY TREASURED

Treat your body, your heart, and your life with as much respect and love as God did when he created you. God created sex too. I'll say that again: God is the designer of sex. He knew what he was doing. But do we?

Sex is so much more than a physical act meeting a physical need. Or maybe I should say that it *should* be so much more, and it can be. Remember, no matter what you've done or where you've been, God offers forgiveness and fresh starts. If you choose to follow God's plan and wait until you're married, sex can still be a fascinating, positive, incredibly special thing for you and your future husband.

What Is Sex?

Sex! This incredible and strange thing seems to be everywhere. It has been written about in poetry with so much depth and compassion since time began. Yet today in TV shows and movies, it's being cheapened. How are we even talking about the same thing?

Talking about sex used to be taboo. In the late 1960s and early 1970s, the sexual revolution came to be. It did help society gain a better attitude or at least the ability to talk openly about sex. Before then, sex wasn't something that was ever mentioned in conversation. But we went from one end of the spectrum to the other and messed everything up again. Although sex has always been an issue, the sexual revolution brought a newfound openness that led to a decline in personal responsibility and commitment. Since then, sex is no longer viewed with the same serious life applications. Here are just some of the statistics:

- Twenty years ago, there were only four sexually transmitted diseases.[1]
- There are now over twenty-five common STDs, and researchers predict the total to be over fifty in the next ten years.[2]
- Half of the infectious diseases in the United States are transmitted sexually.[3]
- One in five of your friends is or will be infected with the human papilloma virus or with genital herpes.[4]
- Eight to 9 percent of teen girls will be pregnant by the age of nineteen, and of them, almost half will get an abortion.[5]

- Today's sexually active female teenager is nine times more likely to suffer from depression, anxiety, and suicidal thoughts or attempts.[6]
- One out of four girls is sexually abused at some point in her life.[7]
- Over half of all pregnant teens get pregnant while using some form of contraception.[8]
- Most teens see over six hundred advertisements in a given day. Over two hundred of them, on average, are selling beauty and sex.[9]

Let's face it, sex is everywhere. I was watching a commercial for tires the other day, and there was a half-naked woman curving through the screen, bending over, making sexual noises, advertising her stomach and legs like she was for sale. After about thirty seconds or so, the commercial finally spoke about how the tires were the best things on the road. To be honest, I'm not sure it ever showed an actual tire!

It's the oldest trick in marketing because it works. Sex is a powerful tool to use if you want to sell something. We think about it, talk about it, see things that remind us of it, and yet we seem to have a hard time understanding it. So what's a teen to do?

Talking About Sex

Sex is the topic that students tend to talk about the most and understand the least. But a funny thing happens when the subject comes up. I ask guys and girls what they think about sex, and what's the first thing they say?

Guys usually say something like, "Uh . . . it's cool." Or, "It's what people do to have a baby." Pretty basic answers, really. Sometimes they don't even know what to say without a little guidance. Guys have to be led around by the hand, so to speak.

Girls usually say things like, "Um . . . that's the only thing guys ever think and talk about." Or, "It's what people do to have babies." Again, fairly simple answers.

No one ever says anything peculiar. Guys will open up about a lot of different things about *some* aspects of sex. They see a lot of it being mocked on TV. A majority of them are exploring the ever-available pornography at their fingertips on computers. Guys can tell you how to physically have sex. They can tell you that good-looking girls and guys love it. They talk about the female body a lot because they see it a lot. They think that sex is about the physical act of having intercourse with the female body so that they can receive pleasure first, and maybe the girl will too.

Sex and Sexuality

A peculiar thing happens as soon as I dip below the surface and ask some deeper questions. The room gets quiet when I ask, "Can you tell me the difference between sex and sexuality? Can you tell me more than two reasons people have sex other than physical pleasure and baby making? Can anyone tell me the difference between love and lust? What's the purpose of marriage beyond having children and living in the same house? What's the percentage of teens who are having sex and regret it?"

Not only are things quiet, but very few guys have opinions that they are confident enough to share with the rest of the class. And those questions aren't even the hard ones.

The Reality of Sex

Sex can be incredibly powerful or it can be exceedingly cheap. It's up to you. One thing that students, especially girls, seem to have a hard time coming to terms with is understanding sexuality. Your sexuality is anything that makes you distinctly female or me distinctly male. Your sexuality is on display all day, every day. You can't help it. We're each going to do things that only males or only females do.

WARNING!

Girls aren't always aware of the ways in which you display sexuality. Most of you aren't learning about how these things are different and what to do about it.

First Comes Love . . . Then Comes Marriage?

When it comes to marriage, let the misunderstandings begin! This is a real tough one. America already has a high divorce rate. That includes Christian Americans! When students are asked about the purpose of marriage, not everyone agrees on the answer.

The reasons often have to do with the type of home we come from. Those situations range far and wide. Many teens come from homes where their dad was never around, or their mom and dad have had a terrible relationship, or teens have been abused, or parents have been divorced, or their mom and dad are never available to them.

It's awful. The reality, however, is that we have to deal with it. If we don't understand the purpose of marriage, how and why are we supposed to know or decide that we aren't going to have sex until we're married? It's a tough question, but a good one.

When it comes to understanding sex and why it should only happen in marriage, we have to think outside the box— or at least that may help. So I try to give teens a more creative path to understanding what sex in marriage is for. So let's all go outside and take a trip in the woods . . .

A Cabin in the Woods: Take One

Imagine that it's a cold winter day. You suddenly find yourself standing in the middle of a forest. You're on your way to a cabin, but it's snowing and getting deep. You've been walking for some time, and now you have to pick up your legs pretty high to step through the deep snow. Your feet are freezing and getting damp. As you breathe in the cold, moist air, it makes your lungs feel like they're burning. Your fingers are getting numb, your ears sting, and you're exhausted!

Finally, in the distance, you see the cabin. You're able to pick up the pace, because you're excited and anxious to get out of the cold. You step up onto the creaky deck and make your way to the door. As you open it up, you instantly feel warmth! You know that inside is a much better place to be. It sure is better than the freezing cold, where your feet and toes feel like they are going to fall off.

As you walk through the door, you immediately notice a large brick wall on the other side of the room. In the center sits a giant fireplace with a big, roaring fire. You shut the door and take a deep breath in and let it out. You smell the cedar wood burning, and it ignites your senses.

You take off your coat, kick the snow off your boots, and lift your freezing feet out of them. It's time to warm your tootsies by the crackling fire. You sit down in a warm, comfortable chair that envelops you as you bask in front of the toasty flames. And what do you drink if you're warming yourself up in front of the fire? Hot cocoa, of course! Well, at least that's what my students almost always say.

What do you have in your delicious hot cocoa? Marshmallows! Why? I think it's because *marshmallow* is a fun word to say, and we love to squeeze those little suckers and watch them float around and make our drinks foam.

Now let me ask you a question. In this little scenario in the cabin, how are you feeling? What are the words that come to mind to describe your feelings in this situation?

Which words would you choose? Usually, students will pick words like *relaxed, peaceful, calm, warm, happy,* and *fuzzy* (they love that word). This is a very happy place to be. The words you think of are positive. The place that has been created is a good place to be.

A Cabin in the Woods: Take Two

Now, let's do this over. You're back in the woods. Once again, you're walking through some deep snow on a cold and cloudy day. Your feet are getting wet and numb. Your legs are tired, and your lungs hurt from breathing in that cold air. Your fingers and ears are freezing and once again, you're exhausted. You look ahead and see the cabin. You trudge through the snow and make your way there. You step onto the deck and open the door.

Inside, you notice a big, roaring fire waiting for you. Except this time, the fire is in the middle of the room next to the couch, burning through the floor! The flames are rising. Smoke begins to fill the room, and within seconds, the couch is ignited. The flames are so large that they are stretching toward the windows and ceiling! In this situation, how are you feeling? Is it warm, cozy, relaxed, happy, and fuzzy? No, it isn't. In fact, those would be ridiculous words to describe the situation. Are you feeling excited, panicky, nervous, frantic, and scared? Any of those words would describe your emotions this time around. This is not a good situation!

Now here's the big question. Can you see how this scenario relates to sex? Maybe, maybe not, so let's take a closer look. Teens usually tell me that they have an entirely different set of thoughts and feelings between these experiences. But I always say that reaction doesn't make much sense. We're still talking about the exact same thing. Nothing has really changed. In both situations it's a cold winter day, there's a cabin in the woods, and a fire in the cabin. So why would they have different reactions to them? The answer, of course, is that one is a controlled environment and the other is not.

Fire!

The only change in our scenarios is the fire. More specifically, where the fire is burning. Yet that one crucial detail either keeps our cabin warm or burns it down. Strangely enough, this is a great analogy for understanding the purpose of sex. The fireplace represents marriage, which is stable, sturdy, and unmoving. It is a strong and lasting place where the "fire" of sex burns. Inside of marriage, sex takes on many more roles. It becomes warm, inviting, safe, comforting, healing, bonding, and secure. **It keeps the house warm.**

Outside of marriage, we don't have a strong and stable environment. There is nothing that we can agree on that lasts. We have engagements, which are a fairly strong indication of marriage. So what happens if we just set our goals on being engaged when we have sex? About 60 percent of engagements don't end up in marriage.[10] So that's not a great idea.

> A successful marriage requires falling in love many times, always with the same person.
>
> —Mignon McLaughlin

There's the idea of living together before marriage. This is becoming a very popular choice today. What about this option? Take a closer look and you'll discover that most people who live together don't end up getting married. Those who do have a much higher rate of divorce. The couple has developed a mentality that if things don't go right they can leave or opt out, so their marriage is less likely to last during difficult times.

What about if you love your boyfriend or you feel like you're ready to have sex? Neither of these ideas produces good results either. First, not everyone agrees on "when love happens." Even more than that, most people don't agree on when they feel ready or prepared to have sex.

That brings us back, once again, to marriage. It is the best and only situation wherein both people are offered a stable and lasting environment. Outside of it, we don't have the same thing.

Does this mean that sex or sexual activity isn't enticing, exciting, and inviting outside of marriage? No. That's the reason many teens end up engaging in it. But it's also very dangerous, and a lot of people end up getting burned. It doesn't keep the house warm; instead, it usually burns it down.

How do we know this? Because high school relationships that engage in sex last an average of less than four weeks. Less than one month after teens start having sex with each other, their relationships usually end. Something that is so great and supposed to bring two people together breaks them apart instead.[11]

Where the fire takes place determines what purpose that fire will serve. Either it will keep that house warm, safe, and cozy—or it will burn it down.

Girls Are the Losers

Let's face it, girls, when it comes to sex, you are the losers. I wish it weren't true, but it is. When it comes to emotions, physical risk, disease, poverty, childbearing, child raising, and most definitely reputation, you wind up as the loser.

If a guy sleeps with a bunch of girls, he's either a stud or people have little opinion of him at all. They definitely don't call him a slut. If a guy was called that, he'd laugh! It would be funny more than it would be hurtful, because it doesn't fit.

Yet if you sleep with even just one guy, you, as the girl, can be called a slut or even a whore.

What about the physical risks of having sex? Girls lose there too. Your reproductive system and parts are all internal. For the most part, a guy's are external. That means from a health standpoint, girls are much more at risk for disease and infection from sexual activity.

Let's take a look at raising babies. It certainly starts with you. You're the one who gets pregnant, has to carry a child for nine months, and then goes through labor to have a child. Eighty percent of guys who get teenage girls pregnant leave them.[12] The average teen mom today gets about sixty-eight bucks a month in child support.[13] Check the food and diaper section at any store, and you'll find that this doesn't even begin to cover the cost of these items in a given month. In fact, about 75 percent of teen moms will live under the poverty line for most of their lives.[14] Their children are three times more likely to do that as well.

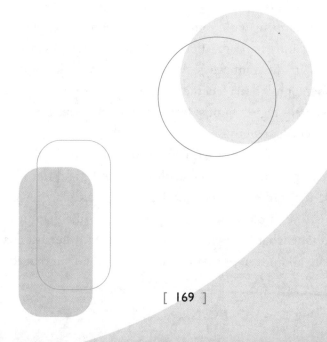

WARNING!

A teenager gets pregnant every thirty-one seconds in this country.[15] Anyone would say that's entirely too many pregnancies. And while this is a tragedy, I have to say that these girls are valiant. It's courageous and admirable for a girl to give up her life to care for her child. Single moms need plenty of encouragement, and they deserve lots of hugs. But there's a better way. Choose not to face any of this stuff to begin with. It's not about just getting by in life; it's about learning how to thrive.

Emotional Gunk

What happens with your emotions when you choose to have sex before marriage? For the most part, sex affects guys and girls in different ways. When it comes to feelings of attachment, guys don't feel the same way at this point in their lives, whereas a girl's brains, feelings, and emotions are more intertwined than a guy's.

A guy can have sex with his girlfriend and then go to basketball practice, hang out with his friends, and not have a single thought about the emotions that took place. A girl is almost the opposite in this respect. She is likely going to think about what happened, talk about it with her friends, and write about it in her journal every night. Given that this type of relationship doesn't usually last for more than a month, she loses once again.

Here is the important part. Despite all of this, guys still need you. After all, who do guys want to marry? Girls! With that said, **if you lose, then guys lose too.** We're all in this together. It's important for us to respect ourselves and also respect you. Likewise, and equally important, it's critical that you respect yourself, your body, your heart, your relationships, and your friendships with us. Just think how much better it could be if you didn't have to worry about any negative consequences in your relationships. Think about how much more enjoyable it would be to live with no regrets and to know that the good decisions you make today are going to bring you far greater happiness later on.

Duct Tape and Bonding

I use duct tape as an example when I talk about sex and how it relates to relationships. I take a roll of duct tape and say, "Sex has the ability to bond people together just like this tape will do to anything it touches." Then I pull out a fairly long piece of duct tape, give it a good rip, and attach it right to my forearm. It's fairly sticky, so it makes a nice loud sound when I say, "I don't think I want this tape here anymore!" and rip it off my arm. It takes little pieces of hair with it and who knows what else off the surface of my arm!

Then I go to another student and put the tape on his arm and rip it off. It still sticks okay, but not as well as it did on mine. Now we have my arm stuff, his arm stuff, and I keep moving on. I go to a few other students, place the tape on their arms, then grip it and rip it. Each time it sticks a little less and picks up little reminders of them. Pretty soon, the tape has so much stuff on it that it doesn't stick to much of anything at all.

WARNING!

When you have sex with someone and that relationship ends, it doesn't really end. You take all that junk from one relationship right into the next. Fear, hurt, jealousy, insecurity, disease, and anything else that is a part of you doesn't just go away. It gets passed on to the next relationship, and the next, and the one after that. If you finally decide to marry someone, you can't bond to him in the same way as you could have.

My point is to leave your duct tape in the drawer until the right time. You need it to bond to the right person at the right time so that the two of you can stick together without any regrets, for life.

18

This Thing Called Love

Love is when the other person's happiness
is more important than your own.

—H. Jackson Brown Jr.

W hat's wrong?" Diane asked her friend Nicole.

"Sam wanted me to have sex with him, and I told him I wouldn't. So he broke up with me!"

"Then he's the wrong guy for you," Diane said matter-of-factly.

Nicole stopped sniffling and looked up in surprise. "What? He's gorgeous! I've been waiting over a year for him to ask me out. Everything was perfect until this happened."

"Then things weren't really perfect," Diane said gently. "Who is more important to you: Sam or the guy you're going to marry someday?" ■

Words That Would Melt Hearts

I find myself trying to sort out what people say about love and sex. I hear so many things. Some of them are funny, some stupid, some cheap, and some good. But I have to think none of them compares to the way God intended love to be—truly romantic and far more powerful and beautiful than any line in a movie.

HERE'S A SECRET:

I'll tell you what guys would love to hear a girl say. It has nothing to do with blowing something up, sports, or movies. It's way better.

Imagine that a guy is standing there with the girl of his dreams ... you. He's a great guy: honest, loving, confident, and committed. As a guy, he would love nothing more than to hear you say, "I have thought about you for so long. I may not have known you or seen you, but you have always been in my heart. As I grew up and had other relationships, I was still waiting just for you. In all the decisions about my heart, I protected it. I did it so that I could love you completely."

Guys would melt if they heard something like that! I sure would. Even if guys don't act like that stuff is important, it is. Guys want a girl who knows two things. First, that she is really valuable. Second, that she thinks he is really valuable too. If you can tell a guy that you thought about him in all of your decisions ahead of time, you are telling him that he is valuable.

> **GUY TIP:**
>
> I wouldn't exactly say this on the first date. (It might really freak him out.) Just know that if you do choose to live your life this way, it will shine through in everything you do and say while you are dating. Then when the right guy does come along, and the moment is right, it will be a beautiful memory that both of you will share forever.

Guys Want to Be Wanted

Underneath all the stuff we've been talking about, there exists something stronger and deeper in a guy's psyche. Sure, guys talk a lot about sex, about feeling good, about all the other reasons that we are so interested in it. There is one thing, though, that is the foundation for all the rest. It's the real driving force behind why guys act the way we do. It's the need to be wanted.

> **NEWS FLASH!**
>
> In surveys about guys' sexual desires, three out of four guys say that if they had all the sex they wanted, they would still be unsatisfied.

When two people fall in love and commit to each other in marriage, something beautiful happens when sex takes place. Two people come together to satisfy each other's needs, wants, and desires. The result is a well-balanced relationship in which both people feel fulfilled.

All guys want someone to tell us that we're strong and caring. Guys need someone to let us know that we are accepted just the way we are and that we can satisfy someone just as we are. That's what a guy wants . . . to show love to a girl and to be loved in return. In a lot of ways, we are just like you!

Take the differences away, and guys and girls are really quite similar! (You're supposed to laugh.) But actually, there's a lot of truth to that statement. How can that be? Because both girls and guys want to give and receive love. Guys and girls both look forward to sharing the special gift of sex that God created for us to share with our spouses. It's the most natural thing in the world to look forward to! It's just a matter of finding the right time, place, and, more important, the right person to share it with.

Don't let yourself get taken in by the wrong guy. Don't let the gift of sex become something cheap. Don't allow yourself to be used, pressured, or intimidated into doing what you want to save for that special someone you'll spend the rest of your life with. If you already have, stop right now! Make smarter decisions from here on. Set your sights and your standards high. It may not be easy, but it will be well worth it. It's up to you. In return, you will be able to offer the most magnificent gift to your spouse on your wedding night. C'mon. There can't be anything more romantic than that!

What's Better Than Sex?

Sex brings people together in six different ways:

1. Physically
2. Emotionally
3. Spiritually
4. Intellectually
5. Socially
6. Morally

These things can't be accomplished outside of marriage. That means that sex in marriage is amazing and purposeful. Outside of marriage, sex is cheap, harmful, and hurtful.

Can sex be enjoyable outside of marriage? Sure, for a few fleeting moments. It obviously brings some enjoyment, or it wouldn't be so tempting. While your parents may be terrified of your knowing that sex can be enjoyable, they really shouldn't worry about that part of the equation. That's because the enjoyment of sex isn't the point of any of this. The fact is, when you're not married, the joy of sex is very short-lived. **Sex outside of marriage makes promises that it cannot deliver.** Sex may try to promise love, but it brings pain instead.

This is a tough subject for me. I'm no angel, and I made a lot of bad and misguided decisions when I was an early teen. I guess you can say that I consider myself "blemished." I made a lot of mistakes with sexual activity and drugs—stuff that was just a cover-up for pain. Although I have changed, and God has fully forgiven me and given me a fresh start, I still have to live with the consequences of the bad decisions I made as a teenager.

There is one thing I can tell you: sex is powerful. Sex is

the TRUTH about GUYS

incredibly important, and yet it is also incredibly overhyped. We spend a very disproportionate amount of time on the subject. We can't have sex all the time. Even if you find the most incredible husband in the universe, you can't have sex all day long. There are a lot of other things you're both going to want and need to do!

Plus, for sex to be as wonderful as possible, you need to be honestly in love and committed to each other—that's much more important than how much you're physically attracted to each other. This is something that guys, especially, have far more trouble understanding in their teens. They are flooded with lust, not love.

There are few things that bring me pure joy: experiencing a sunrise, seeing little kids play, or helping someone just because they need it. A new one on my list? My fiancée. When I get to spend time with her, tell her she is beautiful, tell jokes to make her laugh, or tell her how valuable she is, I feel like I'm on top of the world!

When I get to listen to her dreams about life or I'm just there to listen to the hard stuff, it makes me feel important. When I can give her encouragement and help her understand how wonderfully important the Lord knows she is, it makes me feel like my life is worthwhile. I hope she knows how lucky I feel to be with someone like her . . . wow!

Guess what? All of that is better than sex. Honestly, I'm telling you this kind of relationship is better than sex could ever be. It's seeing the look on her face when she knows I think she's beautiful . . . or when she realizes how much I want to make her happy, because she is so remarkably worth it! Talk about taking your breath away! Believe me, at those moments sex seems very trivial.

Remember, sex is not the house. It's just the thing that keeps things warm once you get inside.

NEWS FLASH!

The biggest message in all of this is to understand the natural progression that relationships should take—from dating to love to marriage to sex. Sex is no substitute for the earlier steps in that progression. Sex can seal, enhance, strengthen, and bond love together. But sex can never be great if love and commitment are not solidly in place to begin with.

Why Wait?

I hope you are seriously rethinking the ways of the world. I hope you understand a little more about how guys think about sex, and I hope you see the horrible consequences of having sex before you're married. Most of all, I hope you see the ultimate joy, hope, and satisfaction you can receive in waiting until you find that one special person who is just for you.

In the Bible, God speaks about being our Father. His role is to love, guide, and protect us. What if he tells us to wait for sex because he has provided a net that can help us know we are loved in a much deeper way first? God cares about you, and he wants to see you smile, not cry.

TOTALLY TREASURED

God wants you to put down the mud that you're playing in and trust him. He has a treasure that he will give you instead. The treasure is something beautiful and won't easily slip away. God wants you to focus on your heart, not your body. You can trust that God's plan is better than your own, and he's working in someone's heart right now as you read this book! He is working to make that heart one that will love you the way you deserve to be loved.

But now it's your turn. A friend of mine once said, "Your heart and body should be so wrapped up in God that a man has to go directly to him to ask for it." Wouldn't that be nice? A guy who asked for directions from the only one who knows the answer?

Just in case you feel like you haven't gotten your fill of advice about this stuff yet, here's some advice from God himself:

Love is patient and kind. Love is not jealous, it does not brag, and it is not proud. Love is not rude, is not selfish, and does not get upset with others. Love does not count up wrongs that have been done. Love takes no pleasure in evil but rejoices over the truth. Love patiently accepts all things. It always trusts, always hopes, and always endures. Love never ends.

—1 Corinthians 13:4–8

This is how God defines love. He wants you to experience this kind of love in the relationship you have with your future husband. You'll notice that this kind of love requires you to be focused on your partner. It's all about giving, rather than self-seeking.

For us to experience this kind of love, we need to first experience God's love for us. Remember, God knows you—everything about you—and he loves you perfectly.

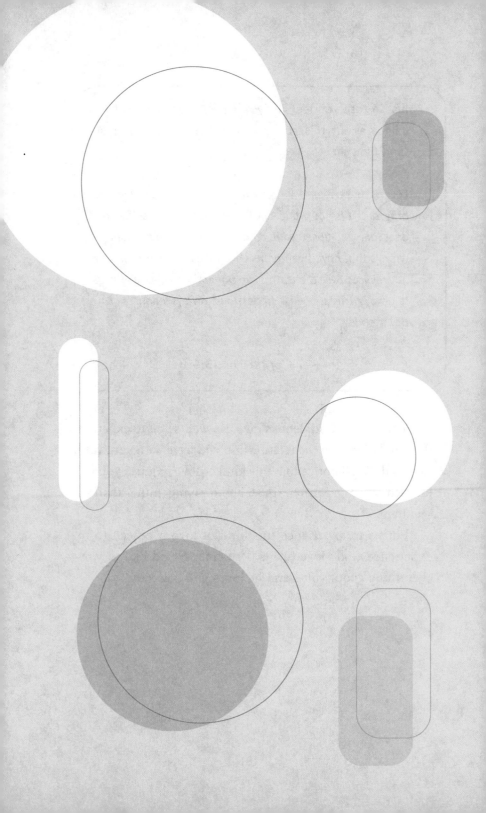

19

Dude Bonding

It is one of those blessings of old friends
that you can afford to be stupid with them.

—Ralph Waldo Emerson

Road Trip!

I thought it might be a little insulting to you if some guy
came along and tried to tell you how to bond. After all, girls
probably bond a lot more, and a lot better, than guys do!

So how do guys bond? I've been
asked this question again and again.
My answer is simple—road trip.

Guys bond differently in the
sense that we connect from the *experiences* we share together. Girls bond
more from the *emotions* you share
with one another.

> Deep experience
> is never peaceful.
>
> —Henry James

Our Comfort Zone

Guys don't want any part of sitting face to face, spilling
our guts to one another. It's just not our choice way to talk.
We need a comfortable—stress on the word *comfortable*—

place to let down our guard. We might play tough, but when it comes to opening up, we get pretty nervous!

Between my junior and senior years of college at Miami University, Ohio, I had a couple of weeks free between summer school and summer camp. Even better, a couple of my best buddies had the time free too. It didn't take us long to have a flash of brilliance, and two words came rushing out— *road trip!* Just like that, it was on.

The Big Adventure

We headed out in an old Honda, just the three of us— Ryan, Luke, and me—ready to tame the wild road. In one week we had planned a pretty wicked road adventure. We made our way from Oxford, Ohio, up the coast of the Great Lakes, through Pennsylvania, to a cottage in New York. From there we were going to hit Buffalo, and then it was on to Niagara Falls and maybe Canada if we had time.

We had a huge list of things to do, and we did every one of them! We drove about fifteen hundred miles during that week, had all kinds of fun, got into some mischief, slept in weird places, ate some pretty wild food, laughed until our sides ached, and not once . . . not one single time . . . did we listen to the radio.

I probably learned more about my friends in that week than I did during the two years before that. **That's what a road trip does. It gives guys a proper setting in which to bond.** Why? Because we were sitting next to each other, looking at stuff, going places, and it just sort of . . . happened. It happened in a way that guys are very comfortable with. It was an adventure, something we could experience and accomplish, and it brought us together in the process.

On the Road Again . . .

I remember a lot about that week. I don't know about your run-of-the-mill weeks, but some of mine come and go without me even noticing. But during that week, I saw the beautiful New York countryside on Lake Erie. I sat in an awesome cottage in a tiny and forgotten little town. I ate unusual foods, sat around a campfire, and played on the beach. We posed like sailors on a beached sailboat, and the goofy picture turned out just incredible! Later, I had the picture made into a painting for my friend's wedding present.

We stared at mammoth things for hours at Niagara Falls. We climbed down a ledge of the cliffs and had someone very, very quickly take our picture.

We talked our way into the kitchen at a famous restaurant where buffalo wings were invented. Before we knew it, we were in the kitchen making the wings with the cooks, mixing the sauce, and tossing them into big containers. I don't know how we wound up doing that, but no . . . it wasn't because we hadn't paid our bill.

We talked for nine straight hours as we headed up to Dartmouth, made a handful of friends on campus, walked the historic river, made clay pottery, and went hiking and camping in the New Hampshire mountains. We looked at a bunch of stores dedicated to the works of Dr. Seuss (who went to Dartmouth), played music in the courtyards with some guys we met, and then drove to the little towns in Massachusetts.

> Map out your future—but do it in pencil. The road ahead is as long as you make it. Make it worth the trip.
>
> —Jon Bon Jovi

We saw where they filmed the movies *The Perfect Storm* and *Stuck on You,* and then we visited a two-hundred-year-old village and ate clam chowder while overlooking the ocean. We walked around Harvard, looked at museums, and talked in our best (but terribly pathetic) Boston accents. We listened to subway musicians and sat in on some great jazz. We went to MIT and sneaked into the classroom where they filmed *Good Will Hunting* and wrote funny things on the boards, took our picture, and then ran away. We tossed a Frisbee and casually talked about nuclear physics with the students sitting on the lawns at MIT. (Well, mostly we just agreed with whatever they said.) Then we ran away from there too.

We took in the sights, sounds, and smells of New York

City. We watched a guy dance in the subway, walked through Times Square, ate hot dogs, and got ripped off by street vendors when we bought fake "designer" watches that broke a couple of weeks later. We even learned about some cool Korean customs when Luke's grandparents took us out for a fancy lunch.

We were sleep deprived and ready to go home by the end of the week. But we'd also had the best time of our lives. It was the most intense road trip I've ever taken, and it brought us together.

Don't get me wrong, I'm sure that both guys and girls like road trips. They are fun, and you can act really goofy. That's not the point. **For guys, it's the experience that bonds us together.** It provides a backdrop for "bonding" to take place. It may be strange to girls, but we are definitely not girls, so we really need stuff like this.

20

Filters and Pressure Gauges

When we long for life without difficulties,
remind us that oaks grow strong in contrary
winds and diamonds are made under pressure.

—Peter Marshall

Turn the Switch to Off

There's a huge pressure switch you have to control. It's called popular culture. It's a strong, powerful pressure that can have amazing effects on your life. It's also a huge joke. Sure, we make fun of past trends, yet we religiously follow current trends. That means the joke is on us, because we're just going to end up looking back and saying, "Why did I try so hard with all of that silly stuff?"

Today's culture puts tremendous pressure on girls and guys every day. It affects your clothes, what you say, what you watch on TV, the music you listen to, keeping up with your neighbors, getting invited to the "right" parties, and staying involved with the right friends—even if they take you to the wrong places. There are diet trends, makeup lines, fashion statements, electronic gadgets everyone has to have, and I could go on and on!

Do yourself a favor. Stop. Take a deep breath, and just stop. Now, if you ignored that request, go back and read it again and *do it* this time. Good. Let's continue . . .

Turn those pressure gauges off. Go ahead. Do it! It's important to give yourself permission to just let go. Ask yourself this question: "What am I really missing out on or losing if I just keep them turned off?" (All the crud, pressure, keeping up with who's who, and every other trend out there.)

Did you come up with any good reasons that you should leave them on? If you did, think about it again. The truth is, most of these things are a waste of your very valuable time. They keep you from finding your unique identity.

GUY TIP:

Finding your own special identity is more attractive to guys—especially the right guys.

I recently read a book that talked about getting rid of distractions. The president of the University of Southern California read an article in the *New York Times* that concluded that after a twenty-four-hour day, 99 percent of their articles would never be read again.[1] Essentially, the paper is obsolete in a very short time. Its shelf life doesn't last.

So he decided to do a weird yet cool experiment in his own life. He cut everything out of his life that he could for a six-month period of time. He stopped sending e-mails, reading the paper, and watching TV. He ▼

even stopped listening to the radio, surfing the Web, and talking on the phone—except when absolutely necessary. What did he conclude he was missing out on? Nothing! He didn't miss a single thing.

All those things that seem so important are often just distractions. He came to the conclusion that he resented a lot of those things he had gotten used to before. It's as though people are constantly invading our thoughts and lives without our permission.

Translation: turn off the things in life that you're being told to obsess about, like guys, your appearance, and all that trendy stuff you don't really need. They will do nothing for you. These distractions tell you how to live, what to think, and how to act. Doesn't it make you mad when you think about it? It makes me mad, because I want to be in charge of my life, not controlled like some monkey who sings and dances when he's told to.

Challenge

What are some of the extra things that you feel you must have every day? Can you identify the stuff that takes up a ton of your time and you can live without? Hint: if you do them every day, you probably feel like you can't live without them. (We're not referring to school, work, or going to the bathroom.) Look at stuff like using the computer, the phone, television, car, and so on.

Try cutting out all these extra things for one week. Just

do it. Don't think about it or reason with yourself. Take a break from the monkey show. Stop e-mailing. Who cares if you don't e-mail or instant-message for a week? You can get back to it, and you won't have missed out on life. The most you'll miss is one of those crummy "pass this on to ten people in two minutes or you'll fall down and kill a puppy" e-mails. Here are some other things to try cutting out:

- Talking or text-messaging on the phone
- E-mailing
- Online chatting
- Watching television
- Reading magazines
- Listening to the radio
- Talking about guys, thinking about guys, flirting with guys, dating guys, and anything else revolving around guys
- Partying
- Shopping
- Putting on tons of makeup
- Having your nails done
- Tanning and anything else surrounding the idea of obsessing over your self-image

Give yourself the freedom to take a test run. It's only one week. You'll probably come up with some interesting conclusions. There is one that will be evident very quickly.

You are *not* missing out on anything in particular. A lot of this stuff is not beneficial to you or anyone else. It even blocks your focus on the stuff that does make a real difference in your life—discovering your real self instead of the one being force-fed to you by today's culture.

Making a choice to weed out distractions at this point in your life can have a significant impact on you and your future. It can open fresh new doors to self-discovery that you may not have ever experienced before. It can make your life less stressful. It will allow you to be yourself, to make friends with people who like you for who you are, and perhaps eventually to attract a guy who will also appreciate these things.

HERE'S A SECRET:

Getting rid of distractions is all part of the filtering system that helps you find the real you. In return, the right person will find you back. You'll learn to identify and avoid unnecessary distractions that will allow you to enjoy a much better life. Exercise this filtering muscle now so it will be stronger in the future.

The Internet

All of the world's information is at our fingertips, and what do we do? We spend hours of time instant-messaging and talking with one another about nothing, day after day on the Internet. We sure haven't solved world hunger or cured any disease because of an instant message. And guess what? We're not going to!

This is relatively short and simple: don't waste much time online. I realize this is just my opinion, but there are important things girls should know about guys when it comes to the Internet. Much like TV, unless you're using it for something practical and getting something done, you're better off not wasting your time on it.

Girls, here is a little Internet information as it relates to guys. It's an easy way out for guys to learn about you with little or no effort. Plus, the Internet and reality are two completely different places. One is fun and there's nothing to lose; the other is a big gamble.

The Internet is becoming an increasingly creepy place. In short, it allows guys to become intimate with girls without having to take any risk. If there is something they don't like, they can click out of it, so it always leaves them in control. The Internet is filled with places that lure you in for stuff that seems innocent and fun. There is a popular site that allows you to set up "buddy profiles," and it's littered with sexual pictures and detailed information that entice predators and tempt danger.

Let's face it, we're not exactly using the Internet to solve big problems. **Don't make yourself available online so that guys can look at you and get to know you with the click of a mouse.**

What's so attractive to guys about instant-messaging or sending a text message? Guys can take risks that aren't really risks at all. It's easy to have a false confidence behind a computer screen.

Simple Rules of Thumb

Don't ever let a guy ask you a question on the computer or on the phone that he wouldn't ask you in person. If you let him, he is taking the easy way out. Make it harder than that. Don't be so available, and don't be at his beck and call.

Filters and Pressure Gauges

Make a guy who likes you put on his parachute, take a deep breath, walk to the edge of the cliff, and jump off. In other words, let him show he's willing to risk rejection in order to spend time with you. If he doesn't, then don't waste your time with him in person or on the Internet. The Internet is cheating, and it hurts everyone in the long run.

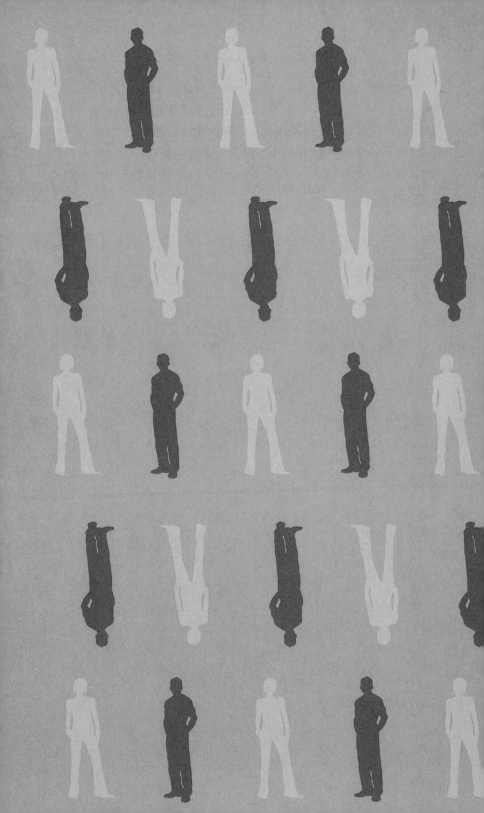

1　2　3　(4)

Other Guy-Girl Things

*Happy is the person
who finds wisdom, the one
who gets understanding.*

—Proverbs 3:13

21

More Stuff Girls Want to Know!

This is my wish for you:
Comfort on difficult days,
smiles when sadness intrudes,
rainbows to follow the clouds,
laughter to kiss your lips,
sunsets to warm your heart,
hugs when spirits sag,
beauty for your eyes to see,
friendships to brighten your being,
faith so that you can believe,
confidence for when you doubt,
courage to know yourself,
patience to accept the truth,
love to complete your life.

—Anonymous

More Stuff You Probably Want to Know

I know this book hasn't addressed every issue you face in life, or even close to it, but, I'll try to do the next best thing. I've included a brief answer to some of the most common questions girls ask me about guys. So here are some of those questions along with my comments and answers about other stuff that might be of interest when it comes to guys and girls.

Q: Do Fish Sleep?

Um . . . I don't know, and honestly, I don't care. I think some of them might. I'll have to look into it. They don't smell good, and I've never really given it a whole lot of thought. So I guess we should move on to the real questions that students ask.

Dating

Q: How do you know what your boundaries should be with someone you are dating?

That's a great question. There are lots of different answers and opinions. I have come across a good principle to live by that seems to answer your question. It's the best rule I've ever heard that actually makes sense. **Don't do anything in private that you aren't okay doing in public.**

I don't mean it's fine if you happen to be a wild and crazy public displayer of affection. I think you get the point. Bring your conscience into play when it comes to the limits. If you have nothing to hide, you're free to get to know one another. It keeps you from having to be sneaky, question your decisions, and defend the stuff you're doing.

The second rule of thumb is to keep your bodies in an upright position when you are with each other. When the two of you decide to go horizontal, it becomes a microwave moment for guys. We go from zero to one hundred in a minute. Getting horizontal usually escalates and takes a couple further than they planned.

The Guy Superiority Factor

Q: *Guys can be real snobs. Why do they assume you have a crush on them if you smile at them more than once?*

Somebody made the mistake of telling guys that God made them the greatest gift to girls. We don't believe it, but we do like ego boosts. If there are guys acting like this, there are a couple of things you can do: (1) let them be, and (2) be nice and go on your way.

Seriously, this is something you don't need to fix. God will deal with our hearts when the time is right. The point for you is that a guy is probably not going to be a good friend or boyfriend if he is too caught up with himself. It's also not your problem, and you should find other things to fill your time.

Guys Can Be Possessive

Q: *Guys want to have their cake and eat it too. They give their girlfriends a hard time about talking to other guys, so why is it okay for them to continue flirting?*

In some cases, I'm sure you are right. If some guys had their way, they would probably stamp "She's mine!" all over every girl they wanted to date or had an interest in. But that's not all guys. It's one of those things that show insecurity. When guys are overly possessive, it shows a lack of confidence. Don't buy into any other explanations. Being possessive is selfish and it's wrong, whether or not it's being done by a guy or a girl. It's also a sign that one or both of you don't have the maturity to be dating anyone just yet.

If a guy is acting that way, it's a sign that he should be by himself, focusing on getting straight with God. If he is insecure because you really are flirting and sending mixed signals, then . . . stop it. This is probably a sign you aren't mature enough to be in a relationship yet either.

Is This the Real Thing?

Q: I have been dating my boyfriend for a long time, and I really feel like he is the one. Is there a good way to know if this is for real?

For fear of sounding like Dr. Phil, I suppose this is a good question. I can't answer specific to your situation, because I don't know you or your boyfriend. But I'll do my best.

Are feelings your only truth meter? If they are, start adjusting now, because life will be confusing if you don't make some changes. Also, I think it's smart for a girl to be overcautious as opposed to naive. Only a few guys in their teens are thinking about marriage.

If you think, *This is true love; we will be together forever, no matter what people say*, then you will probably have some lessons to learn. More than 96 percent of high school relationships don't last, including the ones that were "absolutely going to be together forever." So it's a good idea not to make any assumptions just yet. It will protect you from making some bad decisions. If I sound unromantic, I'm really sorry.

Truth first, romance later. The truth is, you will probably date several guys before you get married, so treat each one with care. Learn from each experience and relationship. Don't look at every relationship as if you are going to wind up getting married. Deal with the facts before you let your feelings take over. Remember, protect your heart, even from your own feelings when you need to. Go into a relationship to have fun and make a good friend. Nothing more. If, by some extremely small percentage, things should progress into marriage, they will. Don't rush them. Be satisfied with friendship while you are in high school. It's more than enough to handle!

Guys Are Pushy About Sex

Q: My boyfriend is really pushy about messing around, and I feel a lot of pressure to have sex or do other physical stuff. I have a hard time saying no because I don't like people to be mad at me.

Wow. There are too many girls in situations like this. First, get out of the relationship right now. You don't have the self-control, self-respect, maturity, or self-confidence you need. One out of four girls is sexually molested in some way during her life.[1] Countless others get put into situations that they shouldn't and don't know what to do about, and they wind up doing things they regret.

Saying no is a very important part of any relationship. It's a skill that you must learn. If you don't, life will be much harder. You can never please everyone, so don't try. Protect yourself first, and then care for others, in that order. You must come first in this equation. Don't be in a relationship that has pressure; it means someone is getting hurt. Good relationships are all about patience, encouragement, and friendship—but not pressure.

Try this. Say, "Let me talk to my parents about it first."

Then pick up your cell phone and call your mom or dad. When they answer the phone, tell them your date wants to have sex with you, and he'd like their permission to do that in addition to possibly getting you pregnant, assuming responsibility for the child, taking care of the medical bills, vowing to be a good husband, and attending all family functions. That usually sends a loud and clear message that any guy will understand.

Guys Think Complimenting Girls Isn't Cool

Q: *All my girlfriends say I look pretty good, but even when I make a huge effort and look my best, none of my guy friends say anything. It's as if they don't want to!*

Simple answer: don't try to look really good because you want people to compliment you. You are usually setting yourself up for failure. What if, for whatever reason, they don't? Does that affect your self-esteem? If it does, you need to go back and look for your image in God's mirror.

While it's nice to receive compliments, they will not and should not create your self-worth, so don't expect them to. God is always there with compliments, and his are usually better than ours anyway.

The other reason is that it takes a lot of confidence for guys to compliment a girl. We may act confident, but we're faking it. It's just one way of showing a guy's lack of confidence, maturity, or simple awareness. Give us time; we'll get there.

Guys Never Make a Commitment

Q: Why do some guys suddenly withdraw from a relationship and say they don't want to be tied down?

It's usually because they realize they aren't able to be in a relationship. Not all guys feel that way, but as teenagers, there is nothing wrong with a guy not wanting a relationship. It's usually because teenage guys realize they aren't mature enough to care about a girl properly.

The wrong part of the equation is to lead a girl on, make promises, or pursue someone they are going to back out on. The good news is that if you protect yourself and use friendship as the long-term guide, you don't have to worry about getting hurt. Remember, it's up to you to protect yourself. In these situations, time is a great tool and probably the easiest. The best thing that teens can do with their teen years is to have good friends. Dating is usually a hassle and short-lived. **Building friendships prepares you for a good marriage relationship later.**

Guys Are Insensitive

Q: Why do guys seem so insensitive toward our feelings?

If you haven't figured this out by now, let me remind you: guys are different creatures. Our sensitivity will change over time as we grow up. Girls are more emotionally aware at younger ages, and they are capable of expressing their thoughts and feelings better. Make friends, not boyfriends, and this stuff will work itself out. Don't force things until the right time.

Guys Think Fighting Shows Their Strength

Q: *I can't stand it when guys boast about their biceps and how tough they are. Why do they try to act so macho?*

When guys saw Mel Gibson fighting for his country in *Braveheart*, we all forgot two things. First, that Mel was fighting a war. Second, that it was a movie.

It seems funny to girls, but guys acting tough or macho is pretty normal. At some point in the teenage years we realize our desire to feel strong, but we aren't sure if we are or not, so we imitate it. We are simply trying to say, "I want to be strong, and I guess maybe this will build some confidence."

The truth is, a guy needs a strong leader in his life to help him build his strength and teach him kindness and compassion at the same time. If guys don't have this (and many don't), then we usually resort to acting goofy. Hopefully, the guys you will be around will look to good men and the Lord to see what a true warrior-poet looks like.

The Guy and Girl Puzzle

Q: *If most guy-girl relationships don't last, what's a good way to have a relationship in high school? Is there any answer?*

While the question sounds pessimistic, I think there are some really good ways to think about it. There is an old saying that goes, "People will remember you by your entrance and your exit." While that may seem vague, I will try to explain.

How you start your relationships will impact the way you end them. This can be good or bad news. That's up to you. If you start things out as friends, you may leave things that way too. If you start out with romance, the flame dies out quickly, and you are left without feelings of deep caring or friendship.

Friendships start slow and gradually build into something comfortable and meaningful. So when you leave the relationship, you will probably still care for that person and his well-being. This is the more unselfish approach. Friendship is a good answer to a lot of the problems that girls and guys encounter. If you're friends, then you have a base of understanding that says, "I care about you and your happiness." And to me, that's a good place to start—and not a bad place to end if and when it does.

You don't just represent yourself in your relationships. You represent your family, your morals, your beliefs, and God. Strive to represent them with the love and respect they deserve. Think about how you want to be remembered, especially when you're filled with questions.

22

Leaving Guy-ville

Writing this book has been a frantic experience for me in some ways. The reason I say that is because I wanted to write down *everything* I had to say. I wanted to cover every topic you'd ever have to deal with as a teen, so you'd understand guys better in every circumstance that comes up in life. I can get as excited as a circus clown, and it makes me want to cram everything I can into a conversation! Of course, my editor wouldn't let me do that. She said something about a ten-thousand-page book costing $200 not really appealing to everyone. I guess I'll have to live with that.

One thing I did realize, though. More than anything else, I have one exceptional wish for you. I wish that you would discover your true beauty and value through a relationship with Jesus Christ, who loves you more than any guy on earth ever could. Let me tell you a little bit about how he changed my life.

My Journey of Faith and Forgiveness

When I was a kid, I focused on being cool. I believed in God and thought Jesus was important, but that didn't do much for me. Jesus never stopped kids from making fun of me at school. He wasn't someone I could eat lunch with, and he never helped me with my homework.

The whole idea of God being love and truth didn't translate from the Bible into my real life. I needed people to like me, I wanted to fit in, and I wanted to know that I wasn't a dork. I never quite made it into the "cool" circle, but my desire to fit in took precedence over everything else.

When I wound up in a detention center and then rehab at age fifteen, I realized my plan wasn't working. I wasn't fitting in, I was saying all the wrong things, I was angry, and none of the girls I wanted to like me ever did. There was obviously something wrong with me. I knew I wanted something better, but I didn't know what that was or how to get it.

Then my life started to change. The people in that rehab center gave me something very valuable: hope that things could be different. I learned about forgiving others and accepting forgiveness from God. I started to realize that I wasn't a piece of junk. And then I remembered how much Jesus had talked about hope and forgiveness. For the first time in my life, he made sense to me in real life.

I had to stop thinking of God as Santa Claus on steroids, monitoring my "naughty or nice" progress. Instead, God was excited to spend a day with me. He was my friend no matter what I did. He said things that make sense today, like care about people the way you want them to care about you. He also said not to steal. And when I think about the things he said, and why he said them, they really make sense. He created me for a purpose, even if I didn't always feel like it. I started to see myself through his eyes as someone who had made mistakes but was forgiven. And I learned about grace—a gift Jesus had lived and died to give me.

I would be lying if I said that I became a perfect Christian. I still wanted to fit in, be good at sports, and get girls to like me. But it was different now. All the things my mom had read to me from the Bible kept popping into my head. I just wasn't sure I believed them enough to completely follow them.

High school went fast. I had good friends at school, and sports gave me a really good way to build confidence. I was part of a really cool youth group, and it was there that I learned about something crucial to understanding what it means to be a Christian. It was *friendship*. My friends at church really, truly cared about me. We tried to see things through Jesus' eyes, and when we did, we were better friends to one another and everyone else.

During my freshman year of college, I came to a very clear crossroads. I went to a school that was a thousand miles away from home. No one knew me, no one was judging me, and nobody was monitoring my lifestyle. In essence, I had a clean slate. I could do whatever I wanted and be whoever I wanted to be. At some point, we all face this very important crossroads. What type of person will we be when no one is looking? Am I acting like a Christian because other Christians are around, or do I truly believe?

I found myself at the foot of my bed late one night, weeping. It wasn't a manly cry or a slow trickle of tears. It was a snot-slobbering, cry-like-a-baby fest. God had been knocking gently on my heart all of those years, and I was finally willing to throw open the door. I didn't fully know where it would lead me, but I knew and believed that Jesus was telling me the truth, and that I wanted to follow him anywhere. That night, I felt a peace and a comfort I had never known. I was clean, forgiven, and loved.

I still make mistakes, but when I go to him, God forgives me and gives me a fresh start. Not only that, but he has given me compassion for others who make mistakes and a desire to help them see their own value as his creation.

You Are Valuable!

When I think back to that time when I was fifteen and alone, there was one critical thing missing in my life— knowing that I was valuable. I just couldn't see it. I had believed a life full of lies about who I was and who I wasn't. Now, I can't imagine going through an entire life thinking that!

People think I have something to offer. More than that, God thinks I have something to offer, or I wouldn't even be here in the first place! Back then, I didn't know that I could help people, be a good friend, or maybe even become a good role model. I didn't know that life could be so hard, yet still be amazing and beautiful. Living an entire life without knowing that would be horribly miserable for anyone. My heart goes out to those who do suffer because they don't know how important and valuable they are.

So the one thing I hope, more than anything else, is that you know and accept that **you belong! You are valuable!** I mean that with all of my heart.

There is no other you. Things that are unique and valuable have another name . . . we call them treasures. God made you his treasure. God made you as a gift for someone else who will value you as a treasure too.

I hope and pray that you will see yourself the way God sees you. I hope you will better understand that when you see yourself and all of your great qualities, others will see you that way too. When you can find and reaffirm your own value, then others can value you as well. That's a gift from God just for you. A guy can't give you that. It's yours and yours alone to recognize and cherish.

> What we are is God's gift to us. What we become is our gift to God.
>
> —Eleanor Powell

I wish you the best in your journey, and may God bless your paths.

Unbelievable . . . but TRUE!

TEEN PREGNANCY

Nearly one million teen girls get pregnant every year.[1]

The United States has the highest rates of teen pregnancy, birth, and abortion in the industrialized world.[2]

Approximately three in ten girls will become pregnant in the United States at least once before the age of twenty.[3]

Children of teens are more likely to do poorly in school, more likely to drop out of school, and less likely to attend college.[4]

Nearly 80 percent of teen boys who father children do not marry the mother of their child and pay less than $800 annually in child support.[5]

Nearly 40 percent of the fathers of children born to teen mothers are age twenty or older.[6]

Every year, there are approximately fifteen million new cases of STDs (forty-one thousand per day; eight thousand of those are teens).[7]

Approximately one in four sexually active teens is infected with an STD.[8]

In the 1960s, only syphilis and gonorrhea were common. Today there are at least twenty-five STDs, and at least eight new pathogens have been identified since 1980, including HIV.[9]

Less than half of adults ages eighteen to forty-four have ever been tested for an STD other than HIV/AIDS.[10]

At least 15 percent of all infertile American women are infertile because of tubal damage caused by pelvic inflammatory disease (PID), the result of an untreated STD.[11]

It is estimated that as many as one in four Americans has genital herpes, yet at least 80 percent of those with herpes are unaware they have it.[12]

Two-thirds of all STDs occur in people age twenty-five or younger.[13]

DRUGS, SEX, AND ALCOHOL

Teens fifteen and older who drink are seven times likelier to have sexual intercourse and twice as likely to have it with four or more partners as nondrinking teens.[14]

Teens fourteen and younger who use drugs are four times likelier to have sex than those who don't.[15]

Teens fourteen and younger who use alcohol are twice as likely to have sex as those who don't.[16]

Sixty-three percent of teens who use alcohol and 70 percent of teens who are frequent drinkers have had sex, compared to 26 percent of those who never drank.[18]

About 75 percent of the men and at least 55 percent of the women involved in acquaintance rapes had been drinking or taking drugs just before the attack.[17]

Teens fifteen and older who use drugs are five times likelier to have sexual intercourse and three times likelier to have it with four or more partners than those who don't.[20]

Seventy-two percent of teens who use drugs and 81 percent of those who use them heavily have had sex, compared to 36 percent who never used drugs.[19]

RAPE

One out of four girls and one out of six boys are sexually abused before age eighteen.[21]

Eighty-six percent of rapes are committed by someone the survivor knows.[22]

Seventy-eight percent of teens do not tell their parents that they have been raped.[23]

About 75 percent of the men and at least 55 percent of the women involved in acquaintance rapes had been drinking or taking drugs just before the attack.[25]

Forty-two percent of assaults happen in the victim's own home.[24]

Girls who are sexually abused often suffer from a traumatic and profound lack of self-esteem. These girls engage in disempowering and self-defeating behaviors, which can propel them into a cycle of prostitution, addiction, drug dealing, and violence.[26]

Thirty-eight percent of date rape survivors are females between the ages of fourteen and seventeen.[27]

Child sexual abuse is more frequent within families than outside families; disabled children are especially at risk of sexual abuse, especially from people they already know.[28]

The average age for the onset of a sexually abusive relationship is six to eight years old.[29]

Fifty-seven percent of rapes occur while out on a date.[30]

In 2003, 83 percent of the episodes of the top twenty shows among teen viewers contained some sexual content, including 20 percent with sexual intercourse.[31]

Sixty-two percent of completed rapes occur by classmates or friends.[32]

More than 70 percent of girls in the juvenile justice system or in shelters have histories of sexual abuse and assault.[33]

One in four sexual assaults takes place in the victim's home, making it the most common place for an assault to take place. Three out of five sexual assaults occur at night, with the largest proportion occurring between 6:00 p.m. and midnight.[34]

On average, music videos contain ninety sexual situations per hour, including eleven "hard-core" scenes depicting behaviors such as intercourse and oral sex.[35]

Seventy-five percent of women raped are between the ages of fifteen and twenty-one. The average age is eighteen.[36]

Girls who watch more than fourteen hours of rap music videos per week are more likely to have multiple sex partners and to be diagnosed with a sexually transmitted disease.[37]

Reports of molestation of very young children are increasing. More than one-third of all child victims may be five years old or younger; children as young as one week old have been molested.[38]

Marketing Sex to Children, from the Campaign for a Commercial-Free Childhood, showed that children are bombarded with sexual content and messages [39]

Before parents raised an outcry, Abercrombie and Fitch marketed a line of thong underwear decorated with sexually provocative phrases such as "Wink Wink" and "Eye Candy" to ten-year-olds.[40]

Forty-two percent of the songs on the top CDs in 1999 contained sexual content—19 percent included direct descriptions of sexual intercourse.[41]

Notes

Chapter 1: Your Noodles—Our Boxes
1. Bill and Pam Farrel, *Men Are Like Waffles—Women Are Like Spaghetti* (Eugene, OR: Harvest House, 2001).

Chapter 4: Mirror, Mirror
1. Michael Strober, PhD, and Meg Schneider, MA, LMSW, *Just a Little Too Thin: How to Pull Your Child Back from the Brink of an Eating Disorder* (Cambridge, MA: Da Capo, 2005).
2. Carol Emery Normandi and Laurelee Roark, *Over It: A Teen's Guide to Getting Beyond Obsessions with Food and Weight* (Novato, CA: New World Library, 2001).
3. Ibid.
4. Margo Maine, PhD, and Joe Kelly, *The Body Myth: Adult Women and the Pressure to Be Perfect* (Hoboken, NJ: Wiley & Sons, 2005).
5. Center for Consumer Freedom, *An Epic of Obesity Myths*, 2005.
6. Centers for Disease Control and Prevention, National Center for Health Statistics, Division of Vital Statistics, various years, http://www.cdc.gov/.
7. Center for Consumer Freedom, *An Epic of Obesity Myths*.
8. Bill and Pam Farrel, *Men Are Like Waffles—Women Are Like Spaghetti* (Eugene, OR: Harvest House, 2001).
9. H. Weinstock, S. Berman, and W. Cates, "Sexually Transmitted Diseases Among American Youth: Incidence and Prevalence Estimates, 2000," *Perspectives on Sexual and Reproductive Health* 36:6 (2004), 10.
10. Michael Strober and Meg Schneider, *Just a Little Too Thin.*

Chapter 7: Who's Your Daddy?
1. John Eldredge, *Wild at Heart* (Nashville: Thomas Nelson, 2001).

Chapter 8: The Five Toughest Questions Girls Ask (And How to Answer Them)
1. Bill and Pam Farrel, *Men Are Like Waffles—Women Are Like Spaghetti* (Eugene, OR: Harvest House, 2001).

Chapter 9: What We Don't Say
1. Leah Ariniello, "Gender and the Brain," Society for Neuroscience, http://web.sfn.org/content/Publications/BrainBriefings/gender.brain.html.
2. Lillian Glass, PhD, *He Says, She Says* (New York: Pedigree, 1993).
3. Nancy Ammon Jianakoplos and Alexander Bernasek, "Are Women More Risk Averse?" *Economic Injury* 36:4 (Oct 1998), 620–30.
4. Sheila Brownlow, Rebecca Whitener, and Janet M. Rupert, "'I'll Take Gender Differences for $1000!' Comain-Specific Intellectual: Success on *Jeopardy*," *Sex Roles* (Feburary 1998).

Notes

5. Bernice Kanner, "Are You a Normal Guy?" *American Demographics* 21:3 (March 1999), 19.

Chapter 11: Guys and Commitment
1. Donald Miller, *Searching for God Knows What* (Nashville: Thomas Nelson, 2004).
2. *Merriam-Webster Online Dictionary,* 2006, s.v. "commitment," http://www.m-w.com/dictionary/commitment.

Chapter 13: Guys Have Secrets
1. Justin Lookadoo, Hayley Morgan, and Hayley Dimarco, *The Dateable Rules: A Guide to the Sexes* (Grand Rapids: Revell, 2004).

Chapter 14: Dating Advice from Guys
1. Robert E. Rector, Kirk A. Johnson, Lauren R. Noyes, and Shannan Martin, "The Harmful Effects of Early Sexual Activity and Multiple Sexual Partners Among Women: A Book of Charts," The Heritage Foundation, 26 June 2003.

Chapter 17: The Reality of Sex
1. Centers for Disease Control and Prevention, National Center for Health Statistics, Division of Vital Statistics, various years, http://www.cdc.gov/.
2. Ibid.
3. Centers for Disease Control and Prevention, *Sexually Transmitted Disease Surveillance, 2004* (Atlanta: U.S. Department of Health and Human Services, 2005).
4. Centers for Disease Control and Prevention, National Center for Health Statistics.
5. Ibid.
6. Robert E. Rector, Kirk A. Johnson, Lauren R. Noyes, and Shannan Martin, "The Harmful Effects of Early Sexual Activity and Multiple Sexual Partners Among Women: A Book of Charts," The Heritage Foundation, 26 June 2003.
7. Robin Warshaw, *I Never Called It Rape: The Ms. Report on Recognizing, Fighting and Surviving Date and Acquaintance Rape* (New York: Harper Perennial, 1994).
8. Centers for Disease Control and Prevention, "Out-of-Wedlock Births Have Risen to a Third of All Births," National Center for Health Statistics, Division of Vital Statistics, various years.
9. Nancy Wilson, *In Pursuit of the Ideal* (Orlando: NewLife Productions, 2003).
10. Centers for Disease Control and Prevention, National Center for Health Statistics.
11. National Campaign to Prevent Teen Pregnancy, 1997. *Whatever Happened to Childhood? The Problem of Teen Pregnancy in the United States.* Washington, D.C.
12. Sheila Brownlow, Rebecca Whitener, and Janet M. Rupert, "'I'll Take Gender Differences for $1000!' Comain-Specific Intellectual: Success on *Jeopardy*," *Sex Roles* (February 1998).
13. The Alan Guttmacher Institute, http://www.guttmacher.org/.
14. Centers for Disease Control and Prevention, "Out-of-Wedlock Births Have Risen to a Third of All Births."
15. The Alan Guttmacher Institute.

Chapter 20: Filters and Pressure Gauges
1. Steven B. Sample, *The Contrarian's Guide to Leadership* (San Francisco: Jossey-Bass, 2002).

Notes

Chapter 21: More Stuff Girls Want to Know

1. United States Department of Justice, Office of the Justice Programs, Bureau of Journal Statistics, "Criminal Victimization in the United States—Statistical Tables Index," http://www.ojp.usdoj.gov/bjs/abstract/cvus/rape_sexual_assault.htm.

Chapter 23: Unbelievable . . . but TRUE!

1. National Campaign to Prevent Teen Pregnancy, analysis of S. K. Henshaw, 2003.
2. M. L. Munson and P. D. Sutton, "Births, Marriages, Divorces, and Deaths: Provisional Data for 2004," *National Vital Statistics Reports* 53:21 (2005).
3. National Campaign to Prevent Teen Pregnancy, "Fact Sheet: How Is the 34% Statistic Calculated?" quoted in S. K. Henshaw, *U.S. Teenage Pregnancy Statistics with Comparative Statistics for Women Ages 20–24* (New York: Alan Guttmacher Institute, 2004).
4. R. A. Maynard, ed., *Kids Having Kids: A Robin Hood Foundation Special Report on the Costs of Adolescent Childbearing* (New York: Robin Hood Foundation, 1996).
5. National Campaign to Prevent Teen Pregnancy, "Whatever Happened to Childhood? The Problem of Teen Pregnancy in the United States," 1997.
6. Ibid.
7. Centers for Disease Control and Prevention, National Center for Health Statistics, Division of Vital Statistics, various years, http://www.cdc.gov/.
8. Ibid.
9. Ibid.
10. Ibid.
11. Ibid.
12. Ibid.
13. Ibid.
14. Robert E. Rector, Kirk A. Johnson, Lauren R. Noyes, and Shannan Martin, "The Harmful Effects of Early Sexual Activity and Multiple Sexual Partners Among Women: A Book of Charts," The Heritage Foundation, 26 June 2003.
15. Denise Holfers, et al., "Adolescent Depression and Suicide Risk: Association with Sex and Drug Behavior," *American Journal of Preventive Medicine* 27:3 (2004).
16. Ibid.
17. Robin Warshaw, *I Never Called It Rape: The Ms. Report on Recognizing, Fighting and Surviving Date and Acquaintance Rape* (New York: Harper Perennial, 1994).
18. The National Center on Addiction and Substance Abuse at Columbia University (CASA).
19. Ibid.
20. Ibid.
21. D. G. Curtis, *Perspectives on Acquaintance Rape*, The American Academy of Experts in Traumatic Stress, http://www.aaets.org/arts/art13.htm/.
22. United States Department of Justice, Office of the Justice Programs, Bureau of Journal Statistics, "Criminal Victimization in the United States—Statistical Tables Index," http://www.ojp.usdoj.gov/bjs/abstract/cvus/rape_sexual_assault.htm
23. Ibid.
24. Ibid.
25. D. G. Curtis, *Perspectives on Acquaintance Rape.*

Notes

26. Robert E. Rector, et. al, "The Harmful Effects of Early Sexual Activity and Multiple Sexual Partners Among Women."
27. United States Department of Justice, "Criminal Victimization in the United States—Statistical Tables Index."
28. United States Department of Justice, Coordinating Council on Juvenile Justice and Delinquency, Prevention Action Plan Update (October 2001).
29. United States Department of Justice, "Criminal Victimization in the United States—Statistical Tables Index."
30. Ibid.
31. Robert E. Rector, et. al. "The Harmful Effects of Early Sexual Activity and Multiple Sexual Partners Among Women."
32. United States Department of Justice, "Criminal Victimization in the United States—Statistical Tables Index."
33. United States Department of Justice, Prevention Action Plan Update.
34. D. G. Curtis, *Perspectives on Acquaintance Rape.*
35. Centers for Disease Control and Prevention, National Center for Health Statistics.
36. National Victim Center and Crime Victims Research and Treatment Center, *Rape in America: A Report to the Nation,* 1992.
37. Centers for Disease Control and Prevention, National Center for Health Statistics.
38. United States Department of Justice, "Criminal Victimization in the United States—Statistical Tables Index."
39. Campaign for a Commercial-Free Childhood, "Marketing Sex to Children," http://www.commercialfreechildhood.org/factsheets/ccfc-facts%20marketing-sex.pdf/.
40. Robert E. Rector, et. al. "The Harmful Effects of Early Sexual Activity and Multiple Sexual Partners Among Women."
41. Ibid.